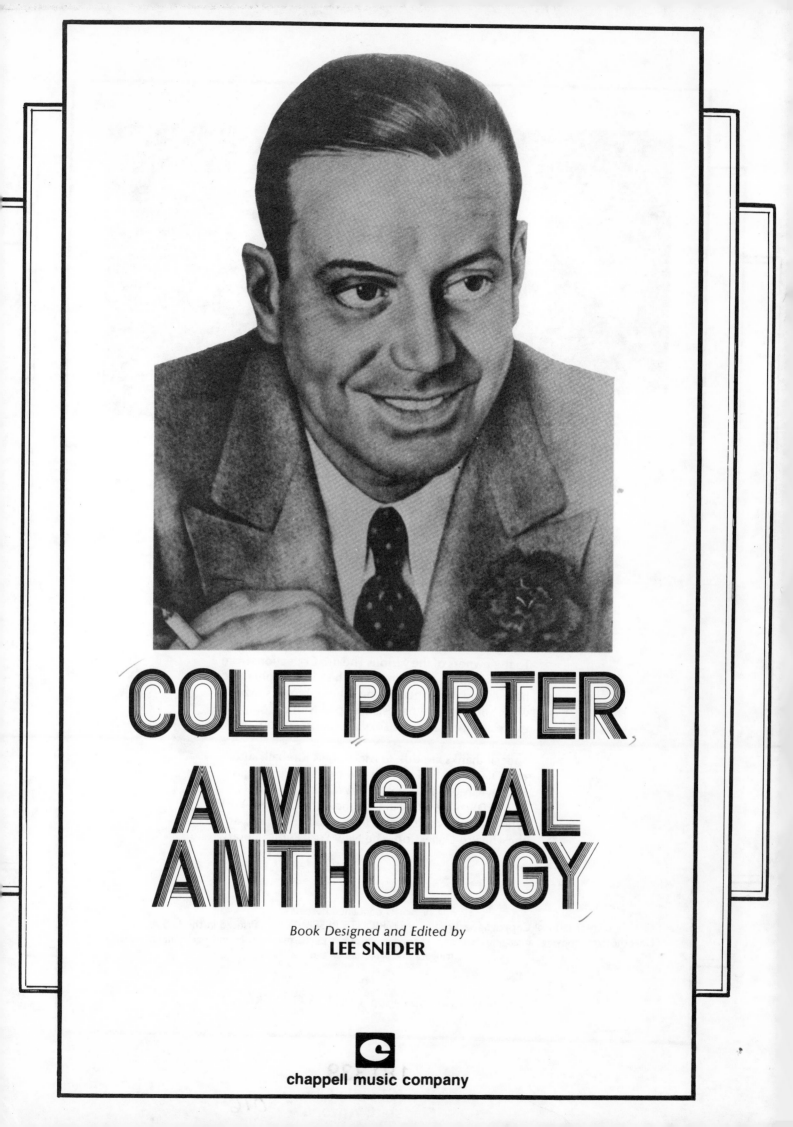

COLE PORTER,
A MUSICAL ANTHOLOGY

Book Designed and Edited by
LEE SNIDER

chappell music company

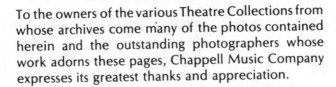

To the owners of the various Theatre Collections from whose archives come many of the photos contained herein and the outstanding photographers whose work adorns these pages, Chappell Music Company expresses its greatest thanks and appreciation.

Special thanks are due to Mr. Robert Kimball, author of COLE published by Holt, Rinehart & Winston; Mr. Stanley Green, author of THE WORLD OF MUSICAL COMEDY; The Museum of the City Of New York (Theatre and Music Collection); Culver Photos; and the Theatre Collection, The New York Public Library.

Production Co-ordination: CHARLES G. RYCKMAN

The SONGS

Cole Porter [signature]

COLE ALBERT PORTER was born June 9, 1893, in Peru, Indiana. His father, Samuel Fenwick Porter, was born in Indiana. He graduated from Indiana University, and is now retired. Mrs. Porter was Kate Cole.

Porter prepared for Yale at Worcester Academy. He was on the Freshman Glee Club, on the University Glee Club three years, and Leader in Senior Year. He was a member of the Dramatic Association, having taken part in "Robin of Sherwood," and written the music for the Smoker Play in 1912 and in 1913. Football Cheer Leader, 1912. Corinthian Yacht Club, University Club, Wigwam and Wrangler Debating Club, Hogans, Whiffenpoofs, Pundits, Grill Room Grizzlies, Mince Pie Club. Delta Kappa Epsilon. Scroll and Key. Freshman Year he roomed alone in 242 York Street; Sophomore Year in 112 Welch; Junior Year in 499 Haughton; Senior Year with H. Parsons in 31 Vanderbilt.

Porter expects to enter the Harvard Law School, after which he will go into either mining, lumbering or farming. His permanent address is Westleigh Farms, Peru, Indiana.

At Yale, 1913: Cole took care to knock two years
off his age (he was actually born in 1891)

COLE PORTER

by ROBERT KIMBALL

This book is a tribute to Cole Porter, one of America's foremost song writers. A courageous man and a great artist, Cole Porter wrote glorious music and sophisticated lyrics that splendidly evoke the times in which he lived yet have endured to bring pleasure to millions and to become a significant part of our cultural heritage. Witty, urbane, ebullient, and poignant, the best Porter songs are crafted with skill, beauty and intensity of expression that bear the subtle and unique qualities of artistic genius.

Here is the most comprehensive collection of Cole Porter songs ever published. Here, too, are the complete lyrics of many songs presented with their music for the first time in the form that most closely approximates Cole Porter's original intentions.

Born in Peru, Indiana on June 9, 1891, Cole Porter was the son of Kate Cole and Samuel Fenwick Porter. He received his formal education at Worcester Academy (1905-09), Yale College (1909-13), Harvard Law and Music Schools (1913-16), and the Schola Cantorum in Paris (1920-21). His

Clockwise (from top left): Cole Porter with a young Tallulah Bankhead; Cole's wife Linda in her garden and on the patio; the Ballroom at Palazzo Rezzonico; the Palazzo Rezzonico in Venice where Cole and Linda passed four summers; Cole at a recording session

musical education, one of the most extensive ever received by an American theatre composer, began under his mother's tutelage with the study of piano and violin. Cole's earliest attempts at composition produced such precocious, albeit pedestrian, concoctions as the *Song of the Birds* (1900) and *The Bob-O-Link Waltz* (1902). His appetite for lyric writing was whetted by his father's avid interest in classic languages and nineteenth century romantic poetry, interests that were further developed in prep school and college.

It was at Yale that he first found his niche as a song writer, creating the famous football songs *Bull Dog* and *Bingo Eli Yale*. His Yale Glee Club specialties (displaying a burgeoning kinship for the lofty heights of the Keith vaudeville circuit) and the musical comedy scores he wrote for his fraternity Delta Kappa Epsilon's initiation plays and the Yale Dramatic Association have been fondly recalled by his contemporaries for their suave, audacious lyrics and captivating music that already forecast the attributes of Cole's later distinction.

Although his Yale triumphs had earmarked him for almost certain success in the theatre, his Broadway debut as the composer and co-lyricist of the comic opera *SEE AMERICA FIRST* in March, 1916 was a fiasco that lasted for only fifteen performances. (Porter had vainly sought to be the American "Gilbert & Sullivan.")

In June, 1917 he sailed for Europe to work with the Duryea Relief Organization but within a few months enlisted in the French Foreign Legion. Later in the War he was attached to the American Embassy in Paris, where on January 30, 1918, at a wedding breakfast in the Ritz Hotel for Ethel Harriman and Henry Russell, he met the exquisite Linda Lee Thomas. Linda, an elegant divorcée whom Bernard Berenson succinctly described as "a great beauty with great brains" and Cole fell in love and were married in Paris in December, 1919.

For a substantial portion of the 1920's Cole and Linda Porter made Europe their home, especially Paris and Venice. They travelled widely and lived and entertained on a grand scale. Linda widened Cole's artistic horizons by introducing him to many outstanding cultural figures as well as leading members of international café society.

One has an almost indelible image of Cole Porter absorbed in his work in the midst of treasure hunts, beach parties, fashionable outings and costume balls. Yet this fabulous, almost unreal world, which would seem on first blush to have a stifling effect on the development of his talent, actually sharpened his satiric gifts, enriched the quality of his art, and inspired some of his most original works.

Yet the 1920's were filled with immense professional frustration for Cole as he was thought by many to be little more than a playboy-expatriate and succeeded in placing only a few songs in stage revues both in London and New York. Nevertheless, buoyed by the constant encouragement of Linda, he continued to work. It is no secret that the songs that seem to us to have been "tossed off" with the most casual effort were in fact the product of a lifelong dedication to his profession and nights and days of the most intense labor.

He worked away from the piano, writing the words and music almost simultaneously. First he created the opening and finish of a song, then proceeded from both beginning and ending toward the middle. The results often produced songs with a special artistic unity, fresh and unhackneyed, and free of many of the cliches of the vast preponderance of the songs of that age. Then, too, Porter was aloof from the mainstream of American life. Living in "exile" in Europe, he maintained some perspective on America's headlong pursuit of material utopia.

Venice: Cole with friends. Note Fanny Brice (seated on left) and Elsa Maxwell (seated, 2nd from left)

Clockwise (from top left): If any characteristic of Cole Porter comes readily to mind it is that of the suave sophisticate, debonair and dapper. Even at work he kept his papers as tidy as his apparel. On his honeymoon in 1921, Porter posed for this amusing photograph by lying in a sarcophagus near the temple of Queen Hatshepsut at Deir el Bahri in Egypt. Porter's love for horses and riding developed as a small boy in his hometown of Peru, Indiana. His grandfather was a multimillionaire and his father the owner of a prosperous drugstore. A trip to South Africa in 1935 gave Cole the opportunity to travel in a rickshaw pulled by a most elaborately costumed chauffeur. Opposite page: Cole Porter and Moss Hart—perhaps invoking the muse?

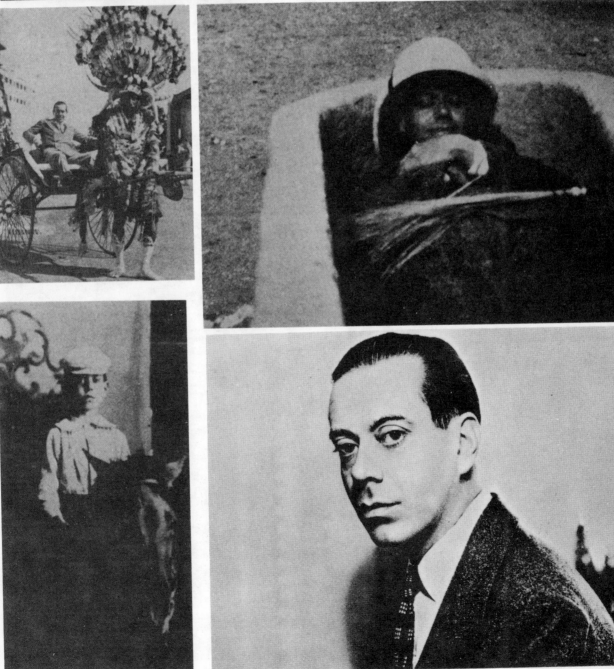

At a recording session

Finally, Porter's creative doldrums — the years of professional frustration after the failure of *SEE AMERICA FIRST* — ended when Monty Wooley asked him to submit songs for a Yale Dramat Christmas show in 1925. A visit to Venice by Fanny Brice in 1927 inspired some additional songs that were sung by Miss Brice at New York's Palace Theatre. Other songs were composed for friends and were performed at private parties. One song, *I'm In Love Again,* became a favorite of bandleaders after they heard it at Bricktop's in Paris and soon Paul Whiteman's recording made it a major success. But the most memorable assistance came from Irving Berlin, Porter's closest friend among theatre composers and a great admirer of Porter's work. He later wrote Cole that "Anything I can do, you can do better," while Porter thought Berlin to be America's best songwriter. Berlin suggested to Ray Goetz, his brother-in-law by a first marriage, that he persuade Cole to write some American songs with a French flavor for Goetz' new show *PARIS.* The show was to premiere at Berlin's Music Box Theatre in 1928 with Mrs. Goetz, the international favorite Irene Bordoni, in a starring role. The rest is theatrical history, as *Let's Do It* was a smash hit and from then on Porter's reputation was firmly established in the front ranks of the theatre.

Unlike the careers of the Gershwins, Rodgers and Hart, Vincent Youmans, DeSylva Brown and Henderson, and countless others, Cole's was no meteoric rise. He did not, as many of them did, come from the ranks of Tin Pan Alley via the traditional route of song plugger, rehearsal pianist, and vaudeville accompanist. His family wealth, while ob-

viating the necessity of seeking this kind of employment, may have been a subtle barrier to his achievement.

With success Porter, in his own words, expanded like "a night-blooming flower." Shows such as *WAKE UP AND DREAM* (1929), *FIFTY MILLION FRENCHMEN* (1929), *THE NEW YORKERS* (1930), *GAY DIVORCE* (1932), *ANYTHING GOES* (1934) *JUBILEE* (1935), *RED HOT AND BLUE* (1936), *DuBARRY WAS A LADY* (1939), and countless others boasted numerous hit songs that buoyed the nation's spirits during the Depression. But it is not true that his most famous songs, *Night And Day* and *Begin The Beguine,* were failures when they were introduced. Nor is it true, as some allege, that Porter's creativity "dried up" after the tragic riding accident he suffered in October, 1937 which required over thirty operations and kept him in constant pain for the remainder of his life. A careful examination of the songs in this book reveals ample evidence of the continuing strength of his creativity.

Cole Porter died on October 15, 1964 and now, almost 12 years after his death, we are in the midst of what many people are calling a "Porter revival." Actually, while Porter's popularity has never waned, it is true that in the past few years his work has become more popular and more admired today than ever before. Hopefully, this volume will refresh the recollections of those who know and love his work and introduce thousands of others to the music and lyrics of a creator who shared his gifts with all of us, who challenged our intelligence, chronicled our foibles, and made us laugh and cry as he touched our hearts.

Mr. Kimball is the author of COLE, published by Holt, Rinehart & Winston.

Red, Hot And Blue

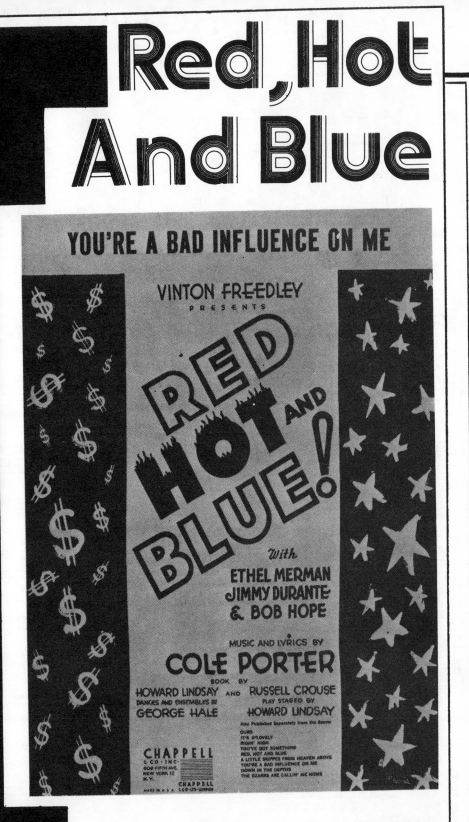

Produced by **VINTON FREEDLEY**

First performance: October 29, 1936 at the
Alvin Theatre, New York
playing for 183 performances

Music & Lyrics by **COLE PORTER**
Book by **HOWARD LINDSAY** and **RUSSEL CROUSE**

Directed by **HOWARD LINDSAY**

The cast included:
Ethel Merman, Jimmy Durante, Bob Hope,
Polly Walters, Grace and Paul Hartman,
Dorothy Vernon, and Thurston Crane

RED, HOT AND BLUE

COLE PORTER

Moderato (Harlem style)

Due to _ the tra - gic low - ness of my brow,_

All mu - sic that's high brow,_ Gets me _ up - set._

Each time _ I hear _ a strain of Stra-

14

-vins - ky's_ I hur - ry to Mins - ky's_

And try_ to for - get. I don't_ like Schu-

- bert's mu - sic or Schu - mann's,_ I'm one_ of those

hu - mans _____ Who on - ly goes in for Ber - lin and Vin - cent You - mans;

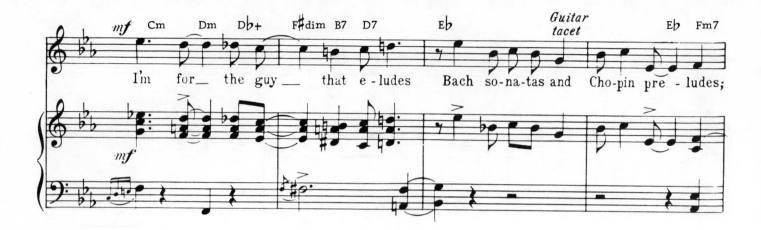

I'm for_ the guy _ that e-ludes Bach so-na-tas and Cho-pin pre-ludes;

So when some nice man I meet,_ I al-ways mur-mur_ tout d'suite.

REFRAIN

If you want_ to thrill me And drill me_ for your

crew, Sing me_ a mel-o-dy_ that's Red, Hot_ and Blue._

Be - fore you_ ex - pand on _ that grand cot - tage for

two, Sing me_ a mel - o - dy _ that's Red, Hot _ and Blue._

I can't take_ Si - be - li - us_ or De - li - us, _

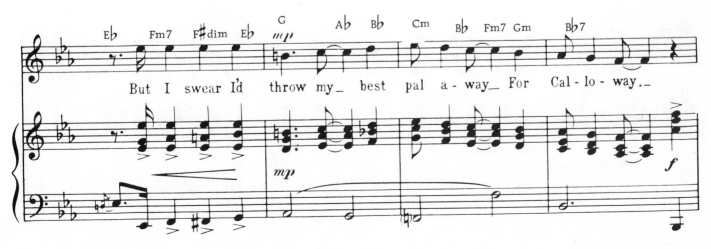

But I swear I'd throw my_ best pal a - way_ For Cal - lo - way._

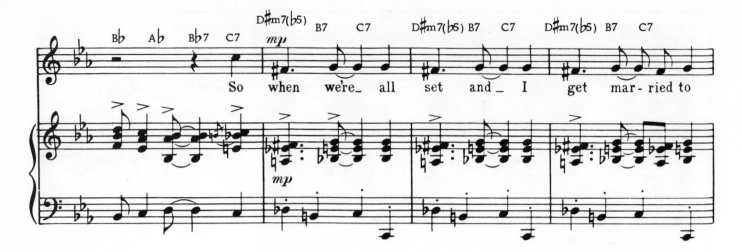

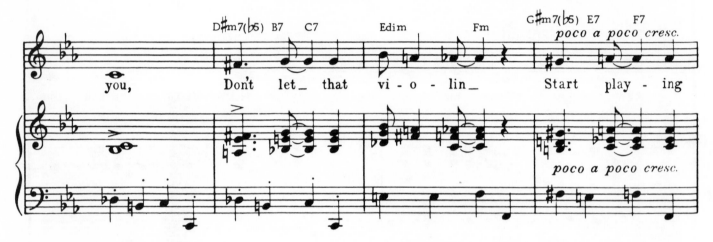

At left: Jimmy Durante, Ethel Merman, and Bob Hope in the 1936 hit RED, HOT AND BLUE. Below: Ethel Merman, center, is reproached by Jimmy Durante, left, while Bob Hope, to Miss Merman's right, looks on in amusement.

DOWN IN THE DEPTHS
ON THE NINETIETH FLOOR

COLE PORTER

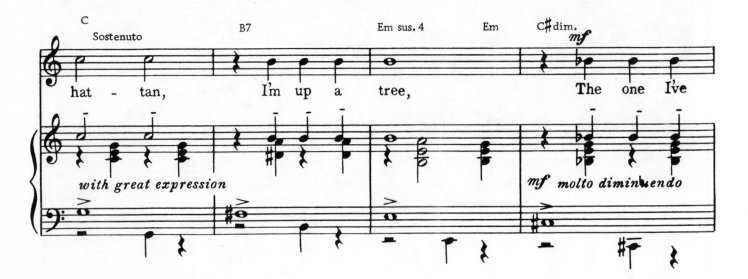

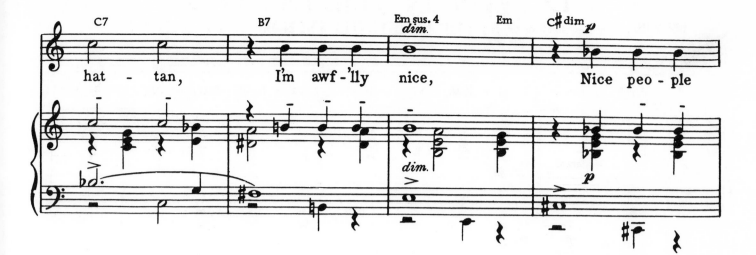

hat - tan, I'm awf-'lly nice, Nice peo - ple

dine with me and e - ven twice. Yet, the

on - ly one in the world I'm mad a - bout Talks of

some-bod - y else,— And walks out.

REFRAIN (Strict slow fox-trot tempo)

With a mil - lion Ne - on rain - bows burn - ing be -

low me, _____ And a mil - lion blaz - ing tax - is rais - ing a

roar, _____ Here I sit a - bove the town, ___ In my

pet pail - let - ted gown, Down in the depths _____ on the

nine - ti - eth floor, _____ While the
While the

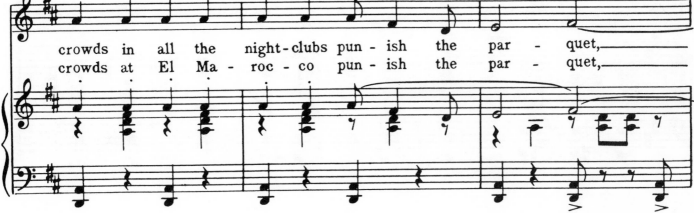

crowds in all the night-clubs pun - ish the par - quet, _____
crowds at El Ma - roc - co pun - ish the par - quet, _____

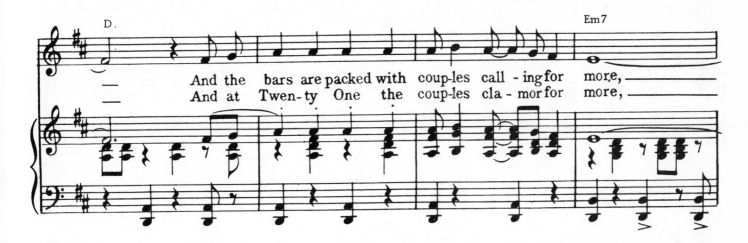

And the bars are packed with coup-les call - ing for more, _____
And at Twen-ty One the coup-les cla - mor for more, _____

I'm de - sert-ed and de - pressed _____ In my reg - al ea - gle

nest, Down in the depths, —— on the nine - ti-eth floor,

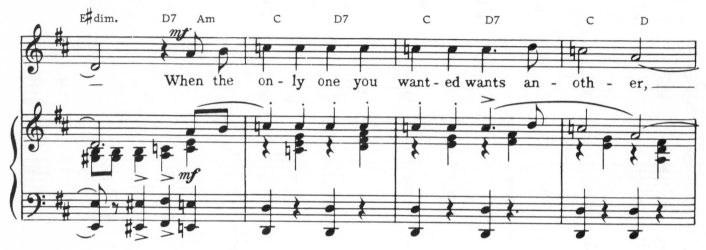

When the on - ly one you want-ed wants an - oth - er, ——

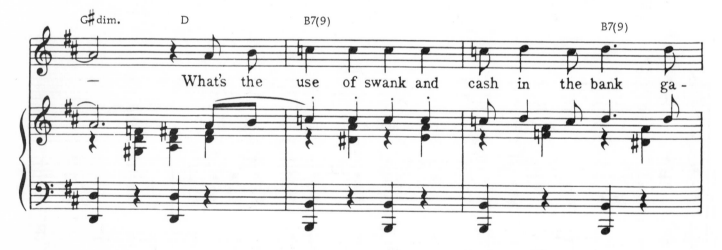

What's the use of swank and cash in the bank ga-

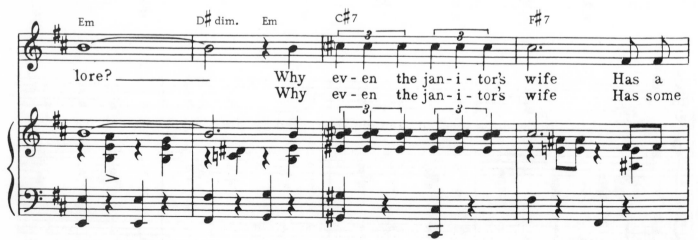

lore? ————— Why ev - en the jan-i - tor's wife Has a
Why ev - en the jan-i - tor's wife Has some

IT'S DE-LOVELY

COLE PORTER

I feel a sud - den urge to sing,— The kind of dit - ty that in-

vokes the Spring, So con - trol your de -sire to curse while I cru-ci-fy the

SHE: This verse I've start-ed seems to me the

Tin Pan-ti-thes-is of mel-o-dy, So to spare you all the

pain. I'll skip the darn thing and sing the re-frain.

HE: mi mi mi mi re re re re, Do sol mi do la si. *spoken* SHE: Take it a-way!

28

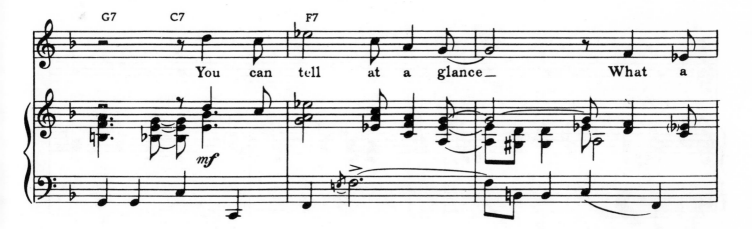

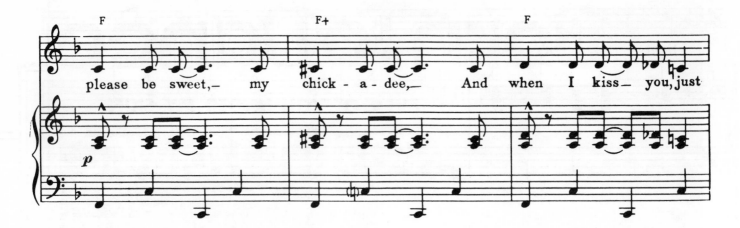

please be sweet,— my chick-a-dee,— And when I kiss— you, just

say to me — "It's de-light-ful,— it's de-li - cious, It's de-

lect - a - ble,— it's de - lir - i - ous,— It's di - lem-ma it's— de-li - mit,

It's ☆ de-luxe, it's de - love - ly."_____ The ___

☆ *Pronounced "delukes."*

Born To Dance

I'VE GOT YOU UNDER MY SKIN

An MGM Film

Produced by **JACK CUMMINGS**

Released in November, 1936

Music & Lyrics by **COLE PORTER**
Screenplay by **JACK McGOWAN** and **SID SILVERS**

Directed by **ROY DEL RUTH**

The cast included:
Eleanor Powell, James Stewart, Virginia Bruce, Una Merkel, Sid Silvers, Frances Langford, Raymond Walburn, Buddy Ebsen, Georges and Jalna, and Reginald Gardner

I'VE GOT YOU UNDER MY SKIN

COLE PORTER

Allegretto Sostenuto

I've got you _____ un-der my skin, _____ I've

got you _____ deep in the heart of me, _____ So

deep in my heart, _____ You're real-ly a part of me. _____ I've

got you _____ un-der my skin. _____ I

tried so _____ not to give in, _____ I

said to my-self,"This af - fair nev-er will go so well." _____ But

why should I try to re - sist when,dar-ling, I know so well _____ I've

got you _____ un-der my skin. _____ I'd

poco a poco cresc. ed appassionato

sac-ri-fice an-y-thing, Come what might, for the sake of hav-ing you near, In spite of a

poco a poco cresc. ed appassionato

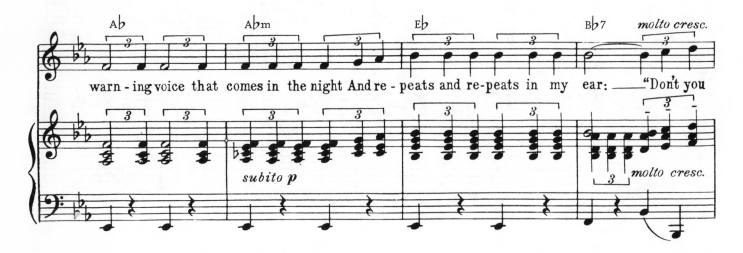

warn-ing voice that comes in the night And re-peats and re-peats in my ear: _____ "Don't you

subito p

molto cresc.

molto cresc.

f molto espressivo

know, lit-tle fool, _____ you nev-er can win, _____ Use your men-

f molto espressivo

34

-tal-i-ty,_____ Wake up to re-al-i-ty." _____ But each

time I do, just the thought of you makes me stop, Be-fore I be-gin, 'Cause I've

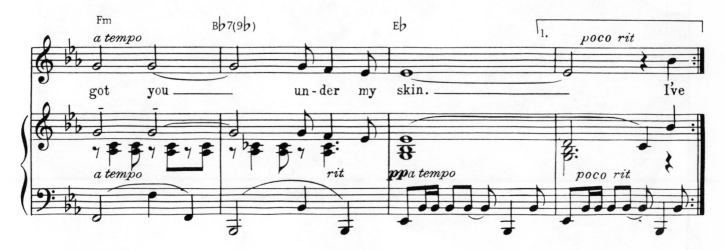

got you _____ un-der my skin. _____ I've

1. Ethel Merman and Bob Hope in RED, HOT AND BLUE.
2. Eleanor Powell dances ''Swingin' The Jinx Away'' in the famous battleship number of BORN TO DANCE. 3. Clifton Webb at the piano, Rex O'Malley in the center, and Libby Holman in YOU NEVER KNOW (1938). 4. Jimmy Stewart perches atop a bench in Central Park while Eleanor Powell demonstrates her dance expertise in BORN TO DANCE. 5. Eleanor Powell dances atop a tier of drums in ROSALIE.

EASY TO LOVE

COLE PORTER

I know too well that I'm ___ just wast-ing pre-cious time in

think-ing such a thing could be, That you ___ could ev-er care for me,

I'm sure you hate to hear____ That I a - dore you, dear, But

grant me, just the same, ___ I'm not en - tire - ly to blame, For

REFRAIN (Slowly, with much expression)

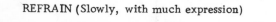

You'd be so eas - y to love, So eas - y to i - dol - ize, all

oth - ers a - bove, So worth the yearn-ing for, ____

So swell to keep ev'ry home-fire burn - ing for, _____ We'd

be so grand at the game, So care - free to - geth-er, that it does seem a

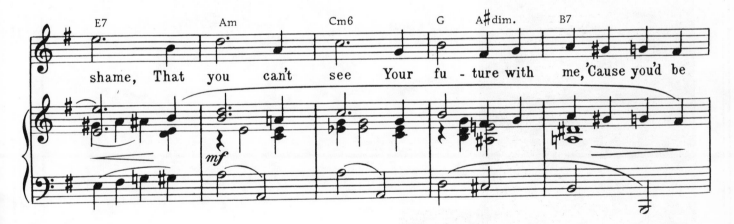

shame, That you can't see Your fu - ture with me, 'Cause you'd be

oh, so eas - y to love! _____ love! _____

Rosalie

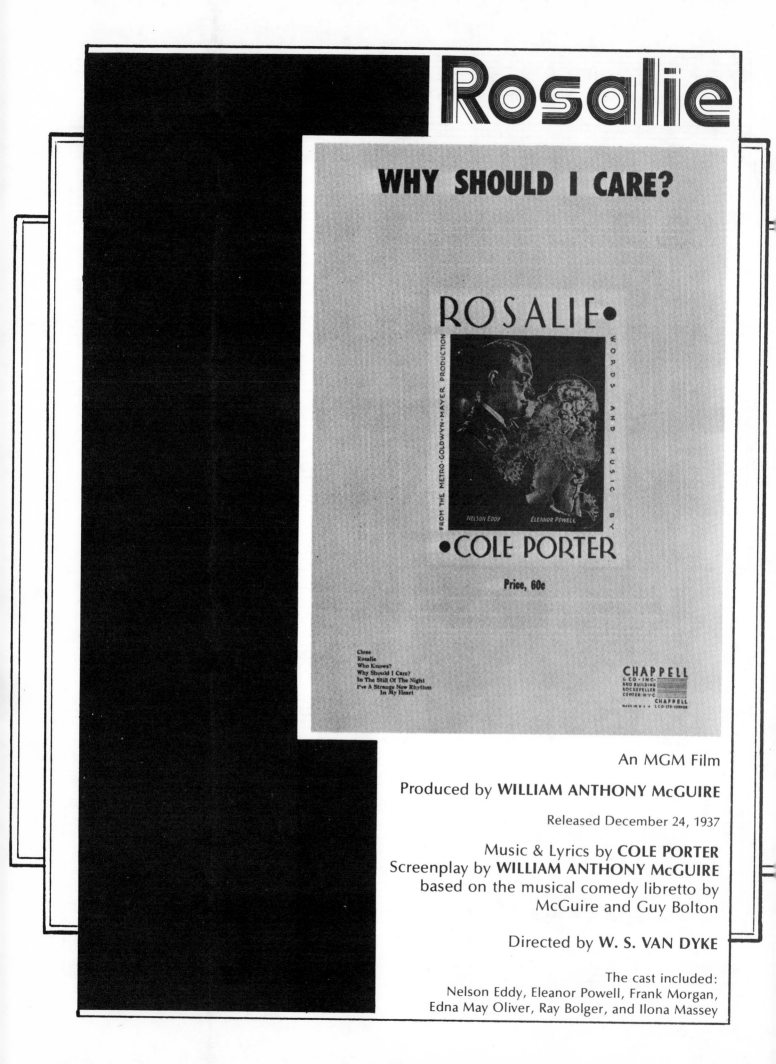

WHY SHOULD I CARE?

ROSALIE •

FROM THE METRO·GOLDWYN·MAYER PRODUCTION

WORDS AND MUSIC BY

NELSON EDDY   ELEANOR POWELL

• COLE PORTER

Price, 60c

Close
Rosalie
Who Knows?
Why Should I Care?
In The Still Of The Night
I've A Strange New Rhythm
In My Heart

CHAPPELL
L·CO·INC·
RKO BUILDING
ROCKEFELLER
CENTER·N·Y·C
MADE IN U S A   L·CO·LTD·LONDON
CHAPPELL

An MGM Film

Produced by **WILLIAM ANTHONY McGUIRE**

Released December 24, 1937

Music & Lyrics by **COLE PORTER**
Screenplay by **WILLIAM ANTHONY McGUIRE**
based on the musical comedy libretto by
McGuire and Guy Bolton

Directed by **W. S. VAN DYKE**

The cast included:
Nelson Eddy, Eleanor Powell, Frank Morgan,
Edna May Oliver, Ray Bolger, and Ilona Massey

IN THE STILL OF THE NIGHT

COLE PORTER

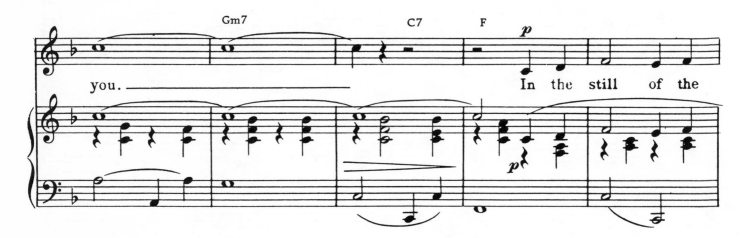

say to you:_____ "Do_____

_ you love me   As I love

you?_____   Are   you   my   life - to -

be,   My   dream   come   true?"_____

Or will this dream of mine fade

out of sight Like the moon, grow-ing

dim, on the rim of the hill

in the chill, Still of the

44

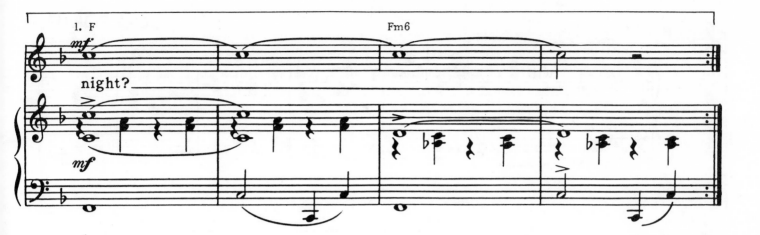

ROSALIE

COLE PORTER

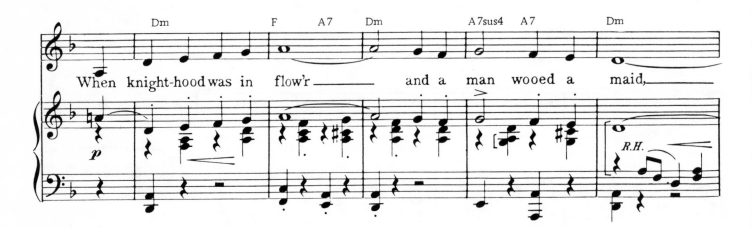

I date,_____ I sup - pose,_____ it's

late,_____ Heav - en knows,_____ it blows_____

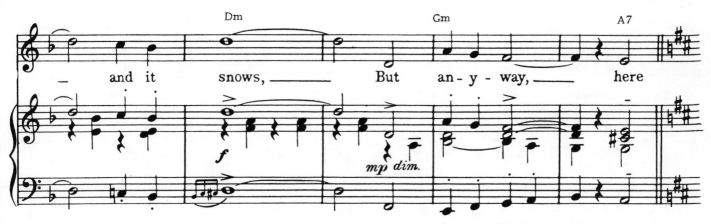

_ and it snows, _____ But an - y - way, _____ here

goes:

REFRAIN (in slow, strict tempo)

Ro - sa - lie, ___ my dar - ling, ___ Ro - sa - lie, ___

___ my dream, ___ Since, one night, ___ When

stars danced a - bove, I'm oh, oh, so much in

love. So, Ro - 'sa - lie, ___ have mer - cy! ___

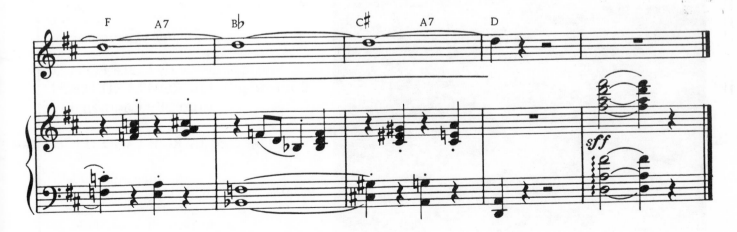

You Never Know

Produced by **LEE & J. J. SHUBERT** in association with **JOHN SHUBERT**

First performance: September 21, 1938 at the Winter Garden Theatre, New York playing for 78 performances

Music & Lyrics by **COLE PORTER**
Book adapted by **ROWLAND LEIGH**
from ''By Candlelight''

Directed by **ROWLAND LEIGH**

The cast included:
Clifton Webb, Lupe Velez, Libby Holman, Toby Wing, Rex O'Malley, Charles Kemper, and June Preisser

AT LONG LAST LOVE

COLE PORTER

I'm ___ so in love, ___ And though it gives me ___ joy in-

tense, ___ I can't de-ciph-er, If I'm a lif-er,— Or if it's

just a_ first of - fense. I'm ___ so in

love,____ I've no sense of val - ues____ left at all._____ Is this a

play - time__ af-faire of May - time, Or is it a wind - fall?____

REFRAIN
Slowly, with warm expression

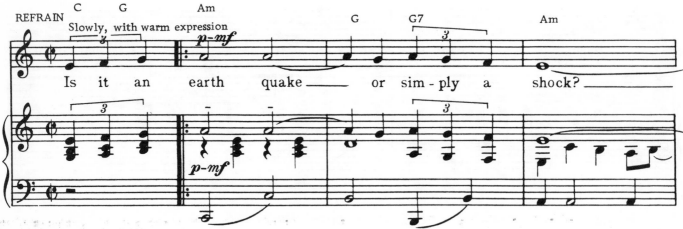

Is it an earth quake____ or sim - ply a shock?____

__ Is it the good tur - tle soup or mere - ly the

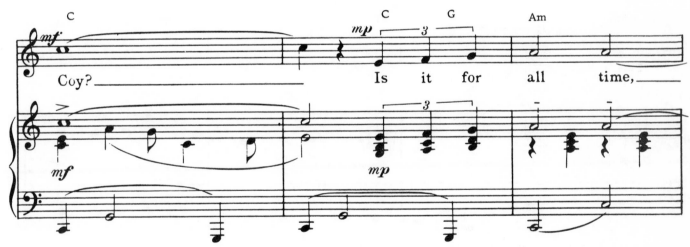

na-da I see or on-ly As-bu-ry Park? _____ Is it a

fan - cy _____ not worth think-ing of, _____

_ Or is it At Long Last

Love. _____ Is it a Love. _____

54

Leave It To Me

Produced by **VINTON FREEDLEY**

First performance: November 9, 1938 at the
Imperial Theatre, New York
playing for 307 performances

Music & Lyrics by **COLE PORTER**
Book by **BELLA & SAMUEL SPEWACK**

Directed by **SAMUEL SPEWACK**

The cast included:
William Gaxton, Victor Moore, Sophie Tucker,
Tamara, Mary Martin, and Gene Kelly

TOMORROW

COLE PORTER

La - dies_ and gen - tle - men, When my heart_ is sick

I've got_ a rem - e - dy_ that does the trick._ So,

la - dies and gen-tle-men, when-ev - er you're blue I ad-

vise you to try_____ My rem-e-dy too,_____ just say:

REFRAIN (Brightly)

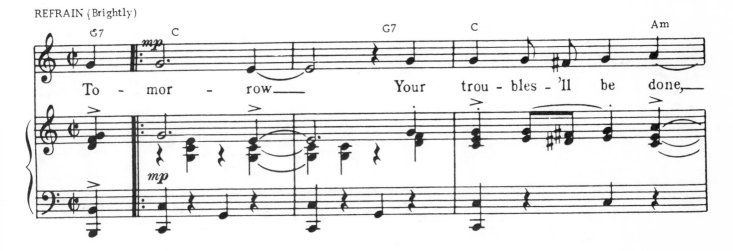

To - mor - row_____ Your trou-bles-'ll be done,_____

To - mor - row_____ Your vic-try-'ll be won,_____

57

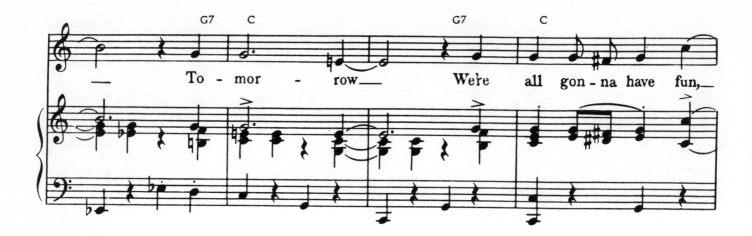

To - mor - row___ We're all gon - na have fun,___

'Cause there ain't gon - na be no sor - row___ to - mor - row.___

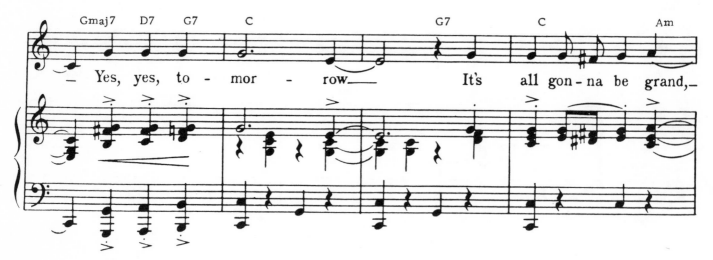

Yes, yes, to - mor - row___ It's all gon - na be grand,___

To - mor - row___ You'll start lead - in' the band,___

58

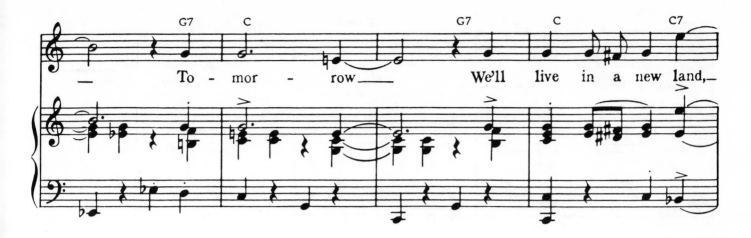

ain't gon-na see____ No clouds in the skies,

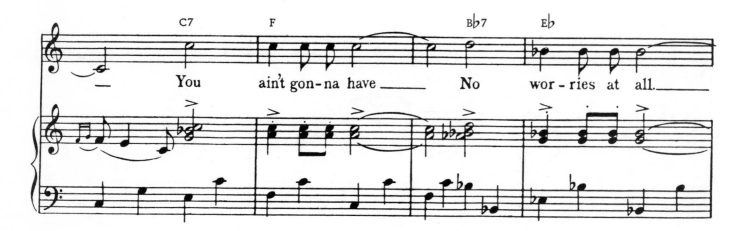

You ain't gon-na have____ No wor-ries at all.____

So why do you fret and get____ your-self ill - er?

You'll feel like a kill-er dill - er. To - mor - row ____

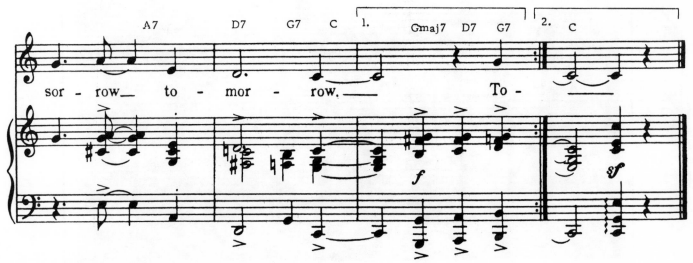

TOMORROW
Complete Version

REFRAIN 1

Tomorrow, your troubles'll be done,
Tomorrow, your vict'ry'll be won,
Tomorrow, we're all gonna have fun,
'Cause there aint gonna be no sorrow, tomorrow.
Tomorrow, when the dawn appears, we all will be so good,
And so intent on doing just exactly as we should,
That there'll be no double crossing, even out in Hollywood,
'Cause there aint gonna be no sorrow, tomorrow.
Tomorrow, you poor Jerseyites, who got such awful jars,
When Orson Welles went on the air and made you all see stars,
I know you'll be relieved to hear we're giving him back to Mars,
'Cause there aint gonna be no sorrow, tomorrow.
Tomorrow, plumpish ladies who are heavier than whales,
Will wake to find that suddenly they're all as thin as rails,
So little Elsa Maxwell will no longer break the scales,
'Cause there aint gonna be no sorrow, tomorrow.
We'll have so much spare time that each of Maurice Evans' plays
Instead of lasting seven hours will last for days and days,
And to make all Federal projects even bigger, we propose
To throw out Harry Hopkins and instead hire Billy Rose.
Tomorrow, this dear world will be so beautiful a place,
And such a happy hunting ground for all the human race,
That you'll even see John L. Lewis with a smile upon his face,
'Cause there aint gonna be no sorrow, tomorrow.

REFRAIN 2

Tomorrow, your troubles'll be done,
Tomorrow, your vict'ry'll be won,
Tomorrow, we're all gonna have fun
'Cause there aint gonna be no sorrow, tomorrow.
Yes, Yes, tomorrow, it's all gonna be grand,
Tomorrow, you'll start leadin' the band,
Tomorrow, we'll live in a new land
 Cause there aint gonna be no sorrow, tomorrow.
There aint gonna be
No tears in your eyes,
You aint gonna see
No clouds in the skies,
You aint gonna have
No worries at all,
So why do you fret yourself iller?
You'll feel like a killer-diller·
Tomorrow, you'll wake up and feel swell,
Tomorrow, you'll start ringin' the bell,
Tomorrow, we're all gonna raise hell
'Cause there aint gonna be no sorrow, tomorrow.
And so why borrow
Even a small cup of sorrow?
Instead, get in your head, mio caro,
There aint gonna be no sorrow, tomorrow.
No, no there aint gonna be
No sorrow for you and me
Tomorrow.

REFRAIN 3

Tomorrow, there'll be nothin' but peace—
Tomorrow, we'll all get a new lease,
Tomorrow, your trousers'll all crease,
'Cause there aint gonna be no sorrow, tomorrow.
Yes, Yes, tomorrow, the soldiers and their kits,
Tomorrow, will put war on the fritz,
Tomorrow, and move into the Ritz,
'Cause there aint gonna be no sorrow, tomorrow.
You girls who adore
New clothes on your backs,
You'll each own a floor
At Gimbel's and Saks.
You boys who are blue,
'Cause always it's true
When you see the girls,
You want to ensnare 'em,
You'll each have a Turkish harem.
Tomorrow, your dear hubby, madame,
Tomorrow, who's colder than a clam,
Tomorrow, will start pushin' a pram,
'Cause there aint gonna be no sorrow,
Tomorrow.

REFRAIN 4

Tomorrow, if blue, laddie, you are,
Tomorrow, 'cause she's gone away far,
Tomorrow, you'll meet Hedy Lamarr,
'Cause there aint gonna be no sorrow, tomorrow.
Yes, yes, tomorrow, dear lady with gray hair,
Tomorrow, if you'd like an affair,
Tomorrow, Bob Taylor'll be there
'Cause there aint gonna be no sorrow, tomorrow.
You're sure gonna meet
The one you'll adore,
Your heart's gonna beat
As never before,
It's all gonna change
From darkness to dawn,
So why do you squeal and feel so darn bitter?
You'll score like a Yankee hitter.
Tomorrow, the season'll be Spring,
Tomorrow, the birdies'll all sing,
Tomorrow, Dan Cupid'll be king,
So there aint gonna be no sorrow, tomorrow.
And so why trouble
Each time a pin bursts your bubble?
Just say, when you feel 'way below par, oh
"There aint gonna be no sorrow, tomorrow."

CODA

No, no there aint gonna be
No sorrow for you and me
Tomorrow.

Mary Martin (on trunk), Gene Kelly to her immediate left

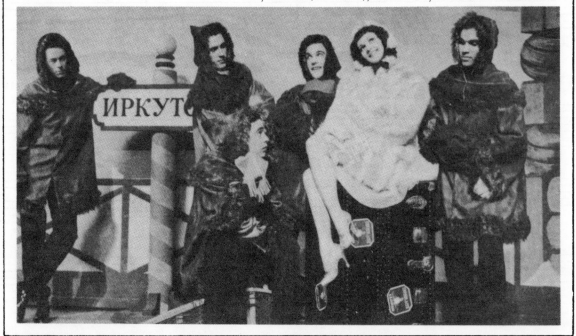

FROM NOW ON

COLE PORTER

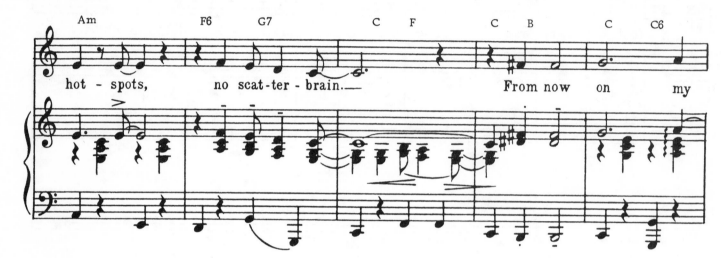

never - er know me ———— When they find I've be-come the

kind Peo-ple call "hom - ey." No more yearn for some - thing

new, dear, My ad - dress is you, dear, From now

on.   From now on. ————

MY HEART BELONGS TO DADDY

COLE PORTER

I used to fall___ In love with all___

Those boys who maul _____ The young cut-ies.___

But now I find__ I'm more in-clined___

To keep my mind_____ On my dut-ies._____ For

since I came to care____ For such a sweet mil-lion-aire._

REFRAIN   Slow Rhumba tempo

While tear-ing off_ A game of golf_ I may make a play for the

cad-dy; But when I do_ I don't fol-low through'Cause my heart be-longs to

Dad-dy. If I in-vite_ A boy some night_ To

dine on my fine fin-nan had-die, I just a-dore_ His

ask-ing for more,_ But my heart be-longs_ to Dad-dy. Yes, my

heart be-longs to Dad-dy, So I sim-ply could-n't be bad. Yes, my

heart be-longs_ to Dad-dy, Da-da, da-da-da, da-da-da - ad! So I

want to warn_ you, lad-die, Tho' I know you're per - fect-ly

swell, That my heart be-longs_ to Dad-dy ___ 'Cause my

Dad-dy, he treats it so well. While well. ___

MY HEART BELONGS TO DADDY

REFRAIN 2

Saint Patrick's day,
Although I may
Be seen wearing green with a paddy,
I'm always sharp
When playing the harp,
'Cause my heart belongs to Daddy.
Though other dames
At football games
May long for a strong undergraddy
I never dream
Of making the team
'Cause my heart belongs to Daddy.
Yes, my heart belongs to Daddy,
So I simply couldn't be bad.
Yes, my heart belongs to Daddy.
Da-da, da-da-da, da-da-da, dad!
So I want to warn you, laddie,
Tho' I simply hate to be frank,
That I can't be mean to Daddy
'Cause my Da-da-da-daddy might spank.
In matters artistic
He's not modernistic
So Da-da-da-daddy might spank.

LEAVE IT TO ME
1. Mary Martin. 2. The Red Square parade with (from left) Tamara, William Gaxton, Victor Moore, Walter Armin, Sophie Tucker, Eugene Sigaloff, Alexander Arso. 3. Sophie Tucker, William Gaxton, Victor Moore.

GET OUT OF TOWN

COLE PORTER

The farce was end - ed, The cur - tains drawn,

And I at least pre - tend - ed That love was dead and gone.

Close to me, dear,— We touch too much..

thrill when we meet Is so bit-ter sweet That, dar-ling, it's get-ting me down.

So on your mark, get set, Get out of

town. ——————————

town. ——————————

DuBarry Was A Lady

Produced by **B. G. DeSYLVA**

First performance: December 6, 1939 at the
46th Street Theatre, New York
playing for 408 performances

Music & Lyrics by **COLE PORTER**
Book by **HERBERT FIELDS & B. G. DeSYLVA**

Directed by **EDGAR MacGREGOR**

The cast included:
Bert Lahr, Ethel Merman, Betty Grable,
Benny Baker, Charles Walters, and Ronald Graham

DO I LOVE YOU?

COLE PORTER

you, I com-posed a tune, _____ So will you lis-ten to it,

dear?

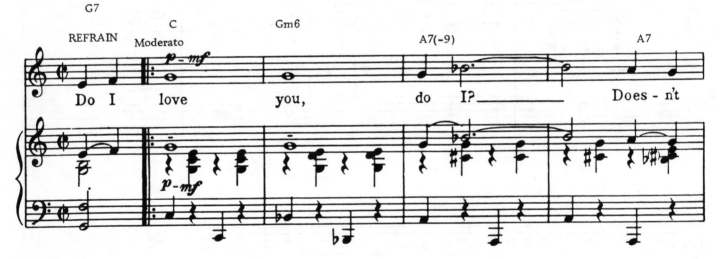

REFRAIN

Do I love you, do I? _____ Does - n't

one and one make two? _____ Do I love

you, do I?_____ Does Ju - ly need a sky of blue?_

_____ Would I miss you, would I,_

_ If you ev - er should go a - way?_____ If the

sun should de - sert_ the day, What would life be?_

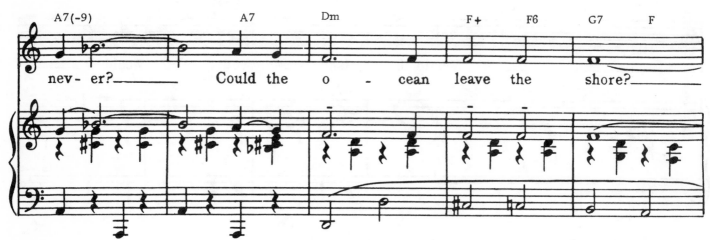

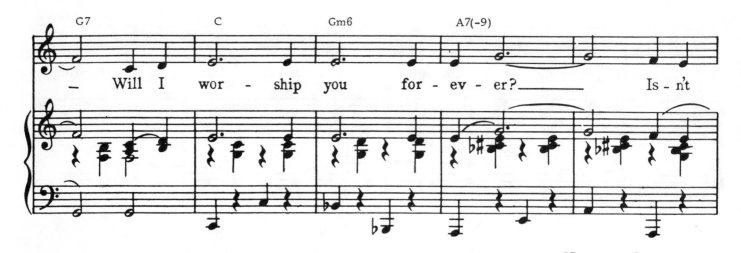

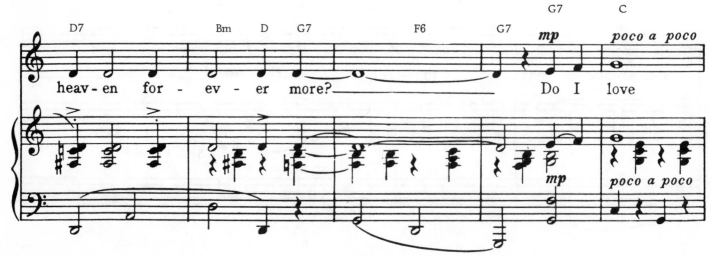

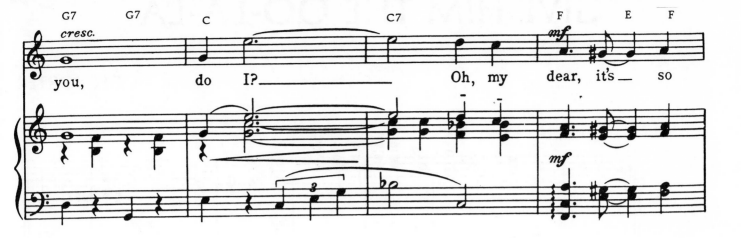

GIVE HIM THE OO-LA-LA

COLE PORTER

Say you're fond of fan-cy things,— Dia-mond clips and

em-'rald rings;— If you want your man to— come through,

Give him the Oo - la - la! When your

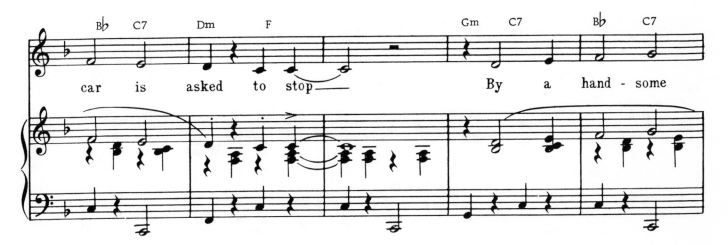

car is asked to stop By a hand - some

traf - fic cop, 'Less you want a tick - et or

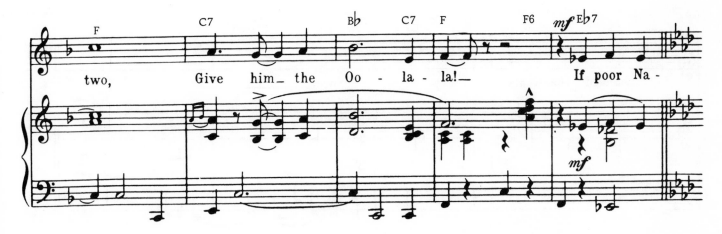

two, Give him the Oo - la - la! If poor Na -

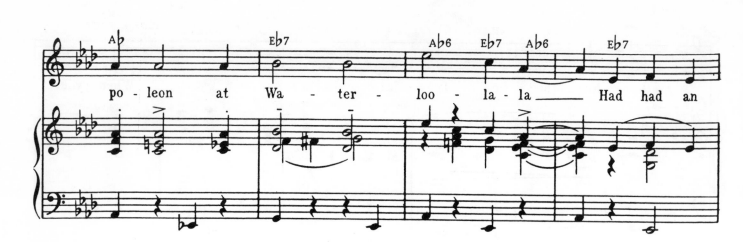

po - leon at Wa - ter - loo - la - la ___ Had had an

ar - my of de - bu - tantes, ___ To give the

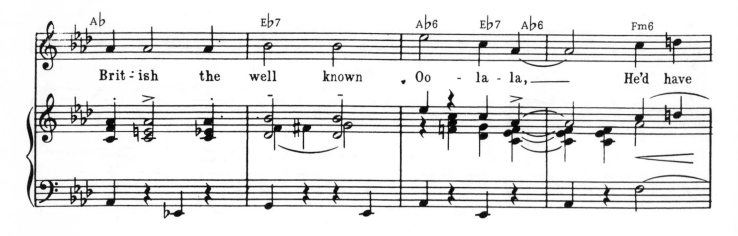

Brit - ish the well known Oo - la - la, ___ He'd have

changed the his - t'ry of France. ___

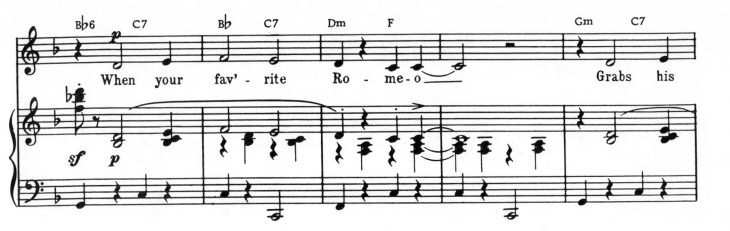

When your fav'-rite Ro - me-o ___ Grabs his

hat and starts to go, ___ Don't re - veal the

fact you_ are blue, Don't break down and start to_ boo-

hoo. There's but one thing for you, la - la, ___

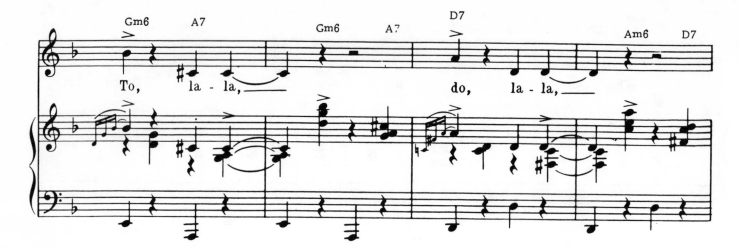

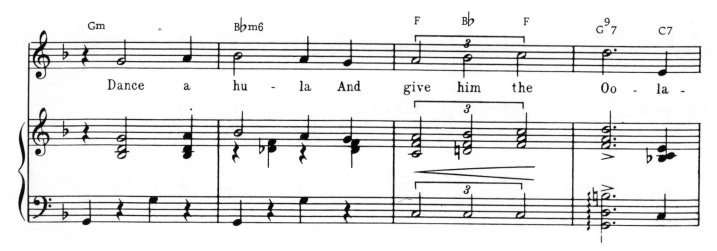

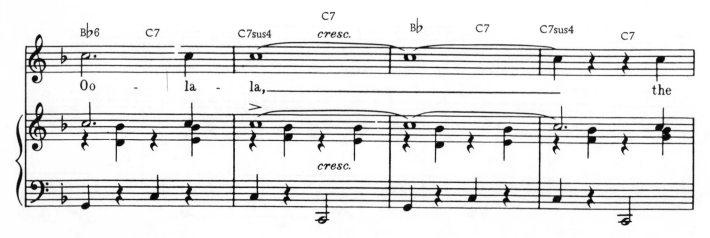

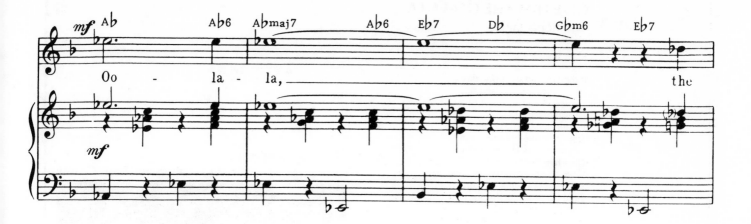

GIVE HIM THE OO-LA-LA
Additional Lyrics

REFRAIN 2

If the tax man calls one day
And insists you pay and pay,
Just to cut your taxes in two,
Give him the Oo-la-la!
If your rich old uncle Ben,
Starts to make his will again,
Just before his lawyer is due,
Give him the Oo-la-la!
If Mr. Roosevelt desires to rule-la-la,
Until the year nineteen forty-four,
He'd better teach Eleanor how to Oo-la-la!
And he'll be elected once more.
If your bridegroom at the church,
Starts to leave you in the lurch,
Don't proceed to fall in a faint,
Don't run wild and crack up a saint,
There's but one thing for you-la-la,
To-la-la
Do-la-la,
Go Tallulah
And give him the Oo-la-la!
La-la, la-la, la-la,
The Oo-la-la,
The Oo-la-la,
The Oo-la-la, Oo-la,
Oo-la-la, Oo-la-la,
Oo-la-la!

Charles Walters and Betty Grable

Bert Lahr and Ethel Merman

IT AIN'T ETIQUETTE
Additional Lyrics

REFRAIN 3

If a very proud mother asks what you think
Of her babe in the bassinette,
Don't tell her it looks like
    the missing link,
It ain't etiquette.
If you're asked up to tea at
    Miss Flinch's school
By some shy little violet,
Don't pinch poor Miss Flinch in the vestibule,
It ain't etiquette.
If you're swimming at Newport with some old leech
And he wrestles you while you're wet,
Don't call him a son of a Bailey's Beach,
It ain't smart,
It ain't chic,
It ain't etiquette.

IT AIN'T ETIQUETTE

COLE PORTER

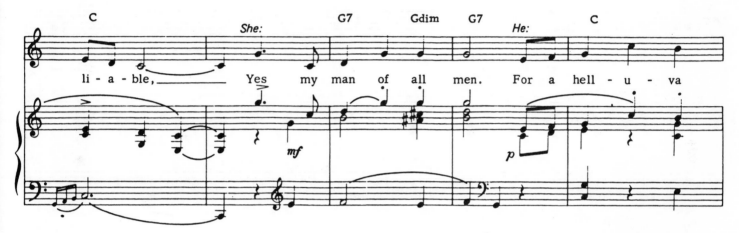

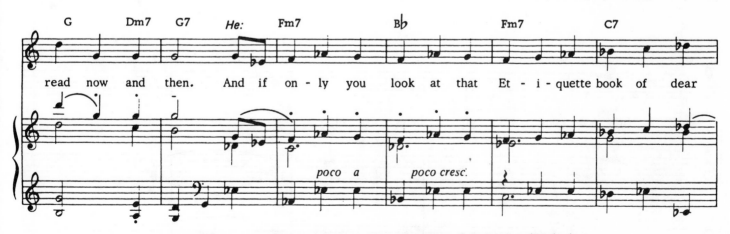

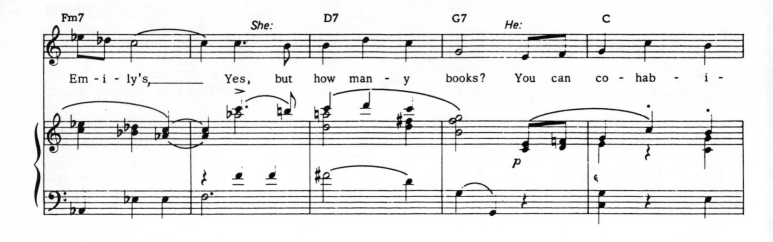

Em - i - ly's, _____ Yes, but how man - y books? You can co - hab - i -

tate with A - mer - i - ca's great fam - i - lies, _____ Now for

REFRAIN

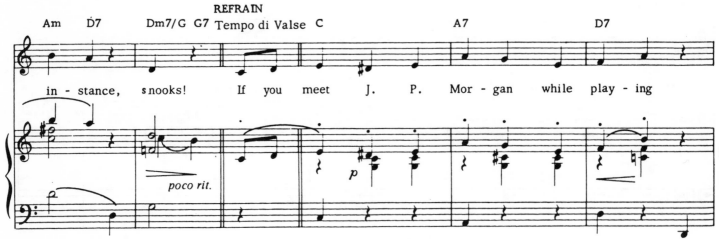

in - stance, snooks! If you meet J. P. Mor - gan while play - ing

poco rit.

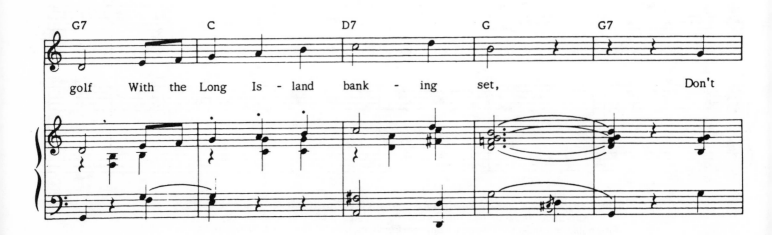

golf With the Long Is - land bank - ing set, Don't

90

greet him by tear - ing your gir - dle off

It ain't et - i - quette! When in - vit - ed to hear from an op' - ra

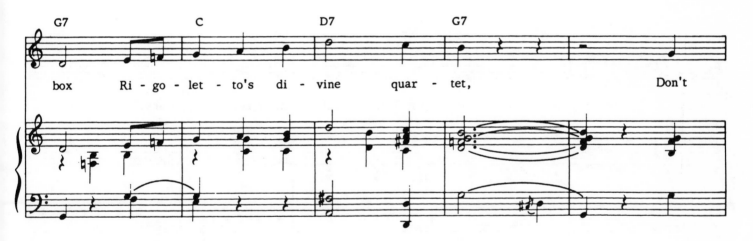

box Ri - go - let - to's di - vine quar - tet, Don't

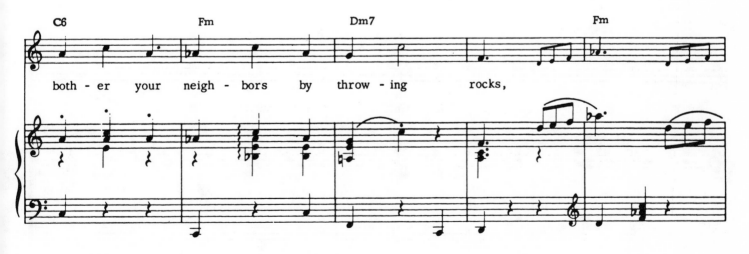

both - er your neigh - bors by throw - ing rocks,

It ain't et - i - quette. When you're asked up to dine by some

mean old minx, And a meat - ball is all you get,

Nev - er say to your host - ess, "This din - ner stinks," It ain't

smart, It ain't chic, It ain't et - i - quette.

WELL, DID YOU EVAH?

COLE PORTER

Moderato (brightly)

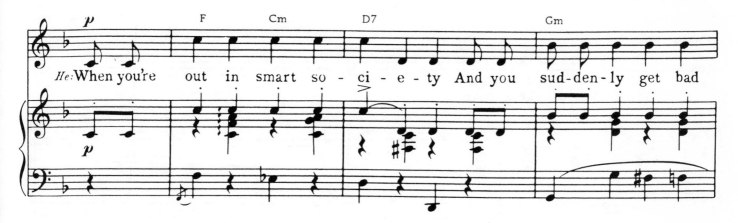

He: When you're out in smart so - ci - e - ty And you sud-den-ly get bad

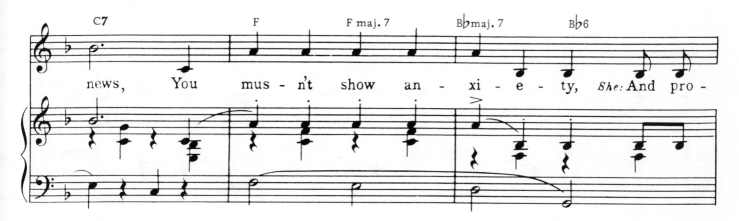

news, You mus-n't show an - xi - e - ty, *She:* And pro -

ceed to sing the blues. *He:* For ex - am - ple, tell me some-thing bad, Some-thing

aw - ful, some-thing grave, And I'll show you how a Rac-quet Club_

lad Would be - have:

REFRAIN

Tempo di Polka

She: Have you heard? The Coast of Maine Just got hit by a

hur - ri - cane? *He:* Well, did you e - vah! What a

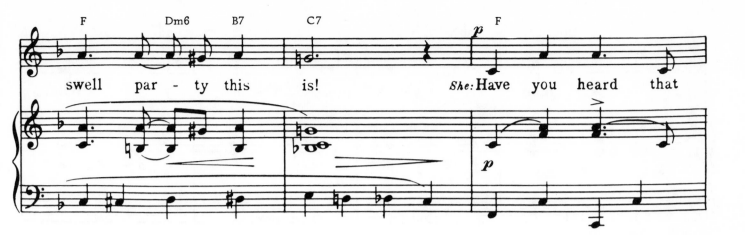

swell par - ty this is! *She:* Have you heard that

poor dear Blanche Got run down by an a - va - lanche?

He: Well, did you e - vah! What a swell par - ty this is! What

Dai - quir - is! What Sher - ry, please! What

Bur - gun - dy! What great Pom - mer - y! What

bran - dy, wow! What whis - key, here's how! What

gin and what beer! *She:* Will you so - ber up, my dear?

Have you heard Pro - fes - sor Munch Ate his wife and di -

vorced his lunch? He: Well, did you e - vah! What a

swell par - ty this is! She: Mis - sus Smith in her new Hup

Crossed the bridge when the bridge was up. He: Well did you e - vah! What a

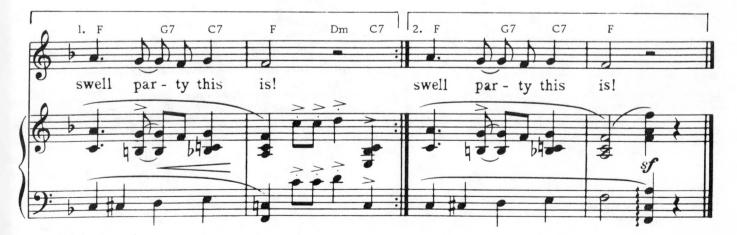

swell par - ty this is! swell par - ty this is!

WELL, DID YOU EVAH?

REFRAIN 1

She: Have you heard the coast of Maine
　　　Just got hit by a hurricane?
He: Well, did you evah! What a swell party this is.
She: Have you heard that poor, dear Blanche
　　　Got run down by an avalanche?
He: Well, did you evah! What a swell party this is.
　　　It's great, it's grand.
　　　It's Wonderland!
　　　It's tops, it's first.
　　　It's DuPont, it's Hearst!
　　　What soup, what fish.
　　　That meat, what a dish!
　　　What salad, what cheese!
She: Pardon me one moment, please,
　　　Have you heard that Uncle Newt
　　　Forgot to open his parachute?
He: Well, did you evah! What a swell party this is.
She: Old Aunt Susie just came back
　　　With her child and the child is black.
He: Well, did you evah! What a swell party this is.

REFRAIN 2

He: Have you heard it's in the stars
　　　Next July we collide with Mars?
She: Well, did you evah! What a swell party this is.
He: Have you heard that Grandma Doyle
　　　Thought the Flit was her mineral oil?
She: Well, did you evah! What a swell party this is.
　　　What Daiquiris!
　　　What Sherry! Please!
　　　What Burgundy!
　　　What great Pommery!
　　　What brandy, wow!
　　　What whiskey, here's how!
　　　What gin and what beer!
He: Will you sober up, my dear?
　　　Have you heard Professor Munch
　　　Ate his wife and divorced his lunch?
She: Well, did you evah! What a swell party this is.
He: Have you heard that Mimmsie Starr
　　　Just got pinched in the Astor Bar?
She: Well, did you evah! What a swell party this is!

REFRAIN 3

She: Have you heard that poor old Ted
　　　Just turned up in an oyster bed?
He: Well, did you evah! What a swell party this is.
She: Lilly Lane has louzy luck,
　　　She was there when the light'ning struck.
He: Well, did you evah! What a swell party this is.
　　　It's fun, it's fine,
　　　It's too divine.
　　　It's smooth, it's smart.
　　　It's Rodgers, it's Hart!
　　　What debs, what stags.
　　　What gossip, what gags!
　　　What feathers, what fuss!
She: Just between the two of us,
　　　Reggie's rather scatterbrained,
　　　He dove in when the pool was drained.
He: Well, did you evah! What a swell party this is.
She: Mrs. Smith in her new Hup
　　　Crossed the bridge when the bridge was up.
He: Well, did you evah! What a swell party this is!

He: Have you heard that Mrs. Cass
　　　Had three beers and then ate the glass?
She: Well, did you evah! What a swell party this is.
He: Have you heard that Captain Craig
　　　Breeds termites in his wooden leg?

Ethel Merman, Bert Lahr in DuBARRY WAS A LADY (1939)

She: Well, did you evah! What a swell party this is.
　　　It's fun, it's fresh.
　　　It's post depresh.
　　　It's Shangrilah.
　　　It's Harper's Bazaar!
　　　What clothes, quel chic,
　　　What pearls, they're the peak!
　　　What glamour, what cheer!
He: This will simply slay you dear,
　　　Kitty isn't paying calls,
　　　She slipped over Niagara Falls.
She: Well, did you evah! What a swell party this is.
He: Have you heard that Mayor Hague
　　　Just came down with bubonic plague?
She: Well, did you evah! What a swell party this is.

FRIENDSHIP

COLE PORTER

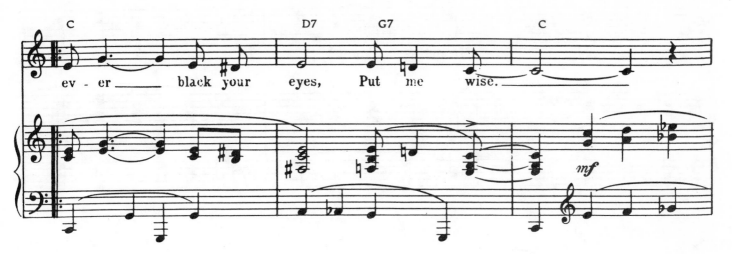

ev - er _____ black your eyes, Put me wise. _____

If they ev - er _____ cook your goose, Turn me loose. _

_ If they ev - er _____ put a

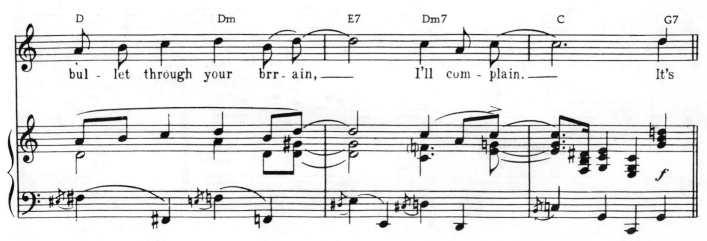

bul - let through your brr - ain, _____ I'll com - plain. _____ It's

friend - ship,— friend - ship,— Just a per - fect

blend - ship.— When oth - er friend - ships have

been for - git — Ours will still be it,— Lah - dle -

ah - dle - ah - dle, hep, hep, hep.— If they —

FRIENDSHIP

Cole Porter's original version

REFRAIN 1

He: If you're ever in a jam, here I am.
She: If you ever need a pal, I'm your gal.
He: If you ever feel so happy you land in jail,
    I'm your bail.
Both: It's friendship, friendship,
    Just a perfect blendship,
    When other friendships have been forgot,
    Ours will still be hot.
    Lahdle—ahdle——dig, dig, dig.

REFRAIN 2

She: If you ever lose your way, come to May.
He: If you ever make a flop, call for Pop.
She: If you ever take a boat and get lost at sea,
    Write to me.
Both: It's friendship, friendship,
    Just a perfect blendship.
    When other friendships have been forgit,
    Ours will still be it,
    Lahdle—ahdle—ahdle—chuck, chuck, chuck.

REFRAIN 3

He: If you're ever down a well, ring my bell.
She: If you ever catch on fire, send a wire.
He: If you ever lose your teeth and you're out to dine,
    Borrow mine.
Both: It's friendship, friendship,
    Just a perfect blendship,
    When other friendships have ceased to jell
    Ours will still be swell.
    Lahdle—ahdle—ahdle—hep, hep, hep.

REFRAIN 4

She: If they ever black your eyes, put me wise.
He: If they ever cook your goose, turn me loose.
She: If they ever put a bullet through your brr-ain,
    I'll complain.
Both: It's friendship, friendship,
    Just a perfect blendship.
    When other friendships go up in smoke
    Ours will still be oke.
    Lahdle—ahdle—ahdle—chuck, chuck, chuck.
    Gong, gong, gong,
    Cluck, cluck, cluck,
    Woof, woof, woof,
    Peck, peck, peck,
    Put, put, put,
    Hip, hip, hip.
    Quack, quack, quack,
    Tweet, tweet, tweet,
    Push, push, push,
    Give, give, give.

REFRAIN 5

He: If you ever lose your mind, I'll be kind.
She: If you ever lose your shirt, I'll be hurt.
He: If you're ever in a mill and get sawed in half,
    I won't laugh.
Both: It's friendship, friendship,
    Just a perfect blendship,
    When other friendships have been forgate,
    Ours will still be great.
    Lahdle—ahdle—ahdle—goof, goof, goof.

REFRAIN 6

She: If they ever hang you, pard, send a card.
He: If they ever cut your throat, write a note.
She: If they ever make a cannibal stew of you,
    Invite me too.
Both: It's friendship, friendship,
    Just a perfect blendship,
    When other friendships are up the crick,
    Ours will still be slick,
    Lahdle—ahdle—ahdle—zip, zip, zip.

Broadway Melody of 1940

An MGM Film

Produced by **JACK CUMMINGS**

Released February 9, 1940

Music & Lyrics by **COLE PORTER**
Screenplay by
LEON GORDON & GEORGE OPPENHEIMER

Directed by **NORMAN TAUROG**
Dance Direction by **BOBBY CONNOLLY**
Art Direction by **CEDRIC GIBBONS**
Costumes by **ADRIAN, VALLES**
Music Direction by **ALFRED NEWMAN**

The cast included:
Fred Astaire, Eleanor Powell, George Murphy,
Frank Morgan, Douglas McPhail, and Carmen
D'Antonio and her vocal group

I CONCENTRATE ON YOU

COLE PORTER

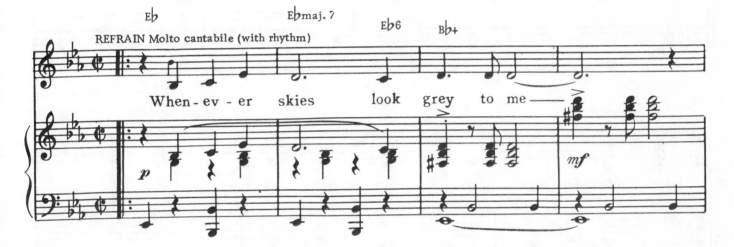

When-ev-er skies look grey to me

And trou-ble be - gins to brew,

When-ev-er the Blues be-come   My on-ly song,

I con-cen-trate on you.   On your

smile   so   sweet,   so   ten-der,   When at

espressivo   *espr.*

first {my {your kiss {you {I de-cline,   On the

light in your eyes, When {you surrender_____ And once a-
{I

gain our arms intertwine._____

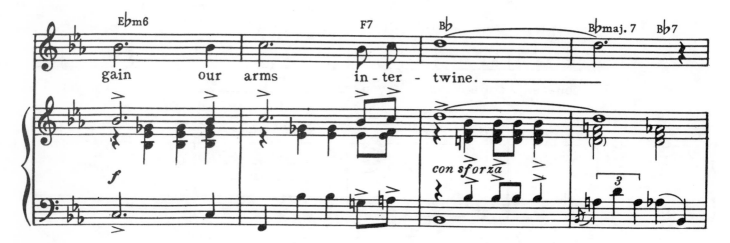

And so when wise men say to me_____

That love's young dream never comes true,_____

To prove that ev - en wise men can be wrong,

mf calmato

poco rit

I con - cen - trate on you.

p poco allarg.

1. Ab6 Eb Bb7

2. Ab6 Eb Fm Bb13(♭9)

I con - cen-trate, ___ and con - cen-trate ___

a tempo *pp*

Bb7 Bb6 Eb

on you. ___

morendo

BROADWAY MELODY OF 1940

Above: Eleanor Powell and Fred Astaire in rehearsal. Opposite page: The special Astaire magic as it appears in the finished version wherein he and Eleanor Powell float through this superb dance sequence. The photos are from the famous "Begin the Beguine" number as the two stars danced on a gigantic mirror which covered 4,000 square feet.

I'VE GOT MY EYES ON YOU

COLE PORTER

date_ down in the dale,_ There's a dic-ta-phone_ Un-der

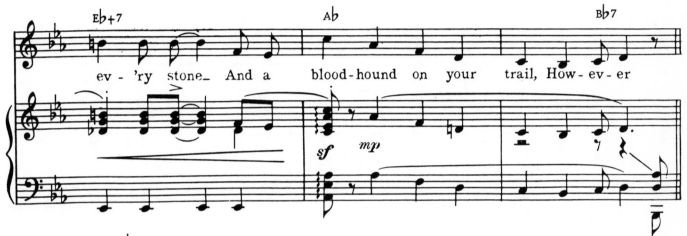

ev-'ry stone_ And a blood-hound on your trail, How-ev-er

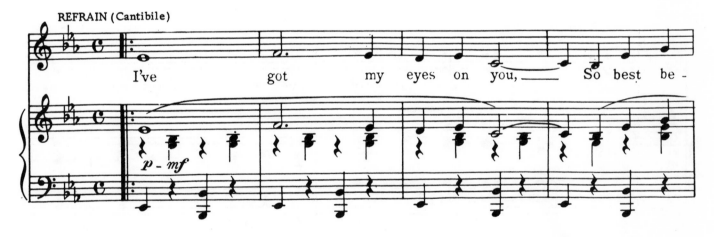

REFRAIN (Cantibile)

I've got my eyes on you,_ So best be-

ware where you roam. _____

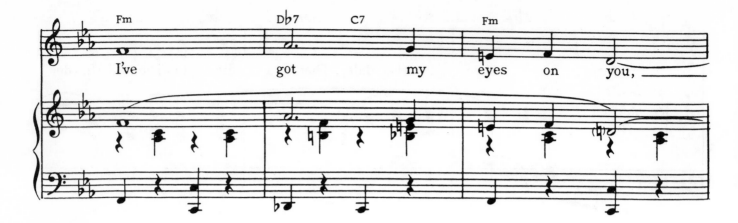

I've got my eyes on you,

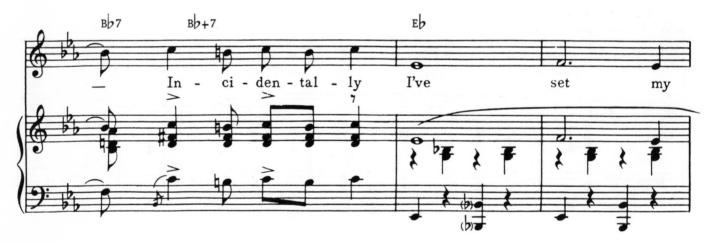

So don't stray too far from home.

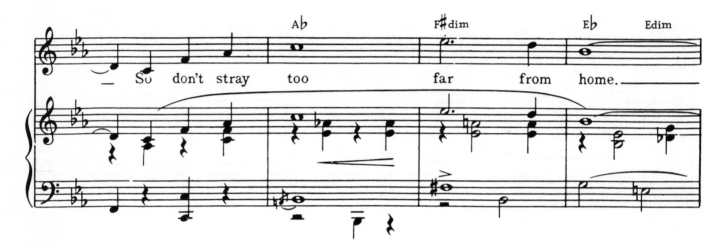

In - ci - den - tal - ly I've set my

spies on you, _____ I'm check-ing on all you do

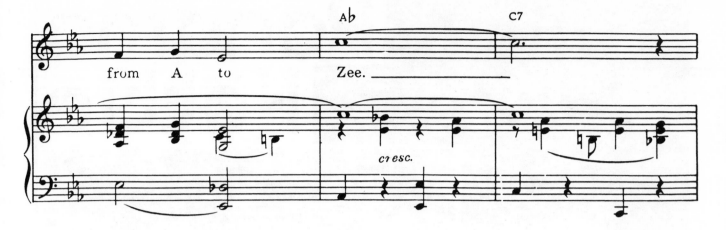

from A to Zee. _____

So, dar - ling, just be wise, _____

_____ Keep your eyes on

me. _____   me.

Panama Hattie

Produced by **B. G. DeSYLVA**

First performance: October 30, 1940 at the
46th Street Theatre, New York
playing for 501 performances

Music & Lyrics by **COLE PORTER**
Book by **HERBERT FIELDS & B. G. DeSYLVA**

Directed by **EDGAR MacGREGOR**

The cast included:
Ethel Merman, Arthur Treacher, Betty Hutton,
James Dunn, Phyllis Brooks, Joan Carroll, Rags
Ragland, Pat Harrington, and Frank Hyers

LET'S BE BUDDIES

COLE PORTER

If you're on the town, If you're on your own, Well I'm sort a

down and sick of be-ing a - lone, Do you ev-er spend your

ev'-nings with the blues? 'Cause if you do, my friend, we're both in the same shoes.

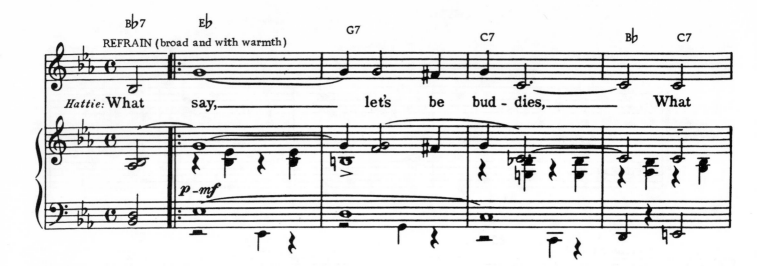

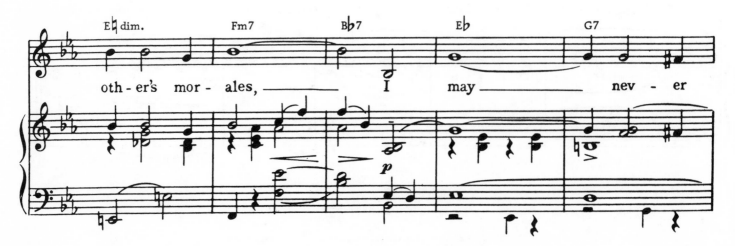

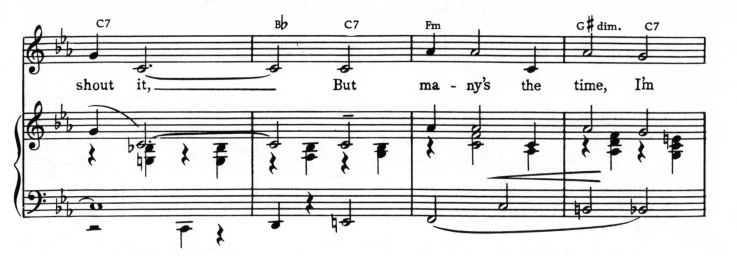

shout it, _____ But ma - ny's the time, I'm

blue, _____ What say, _____ how's a -

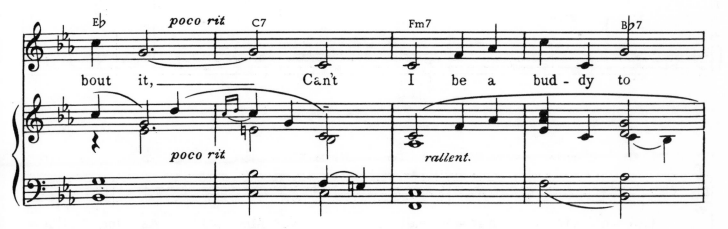

bout it, _____ Can't I be a bud - dy to

you? _____ What you? _____

I'VE STILL GOT MY HEALTH

COLE PORTER

all the same, I'm in the pink,— My con-sti-tu-tion's made of zinc, And you

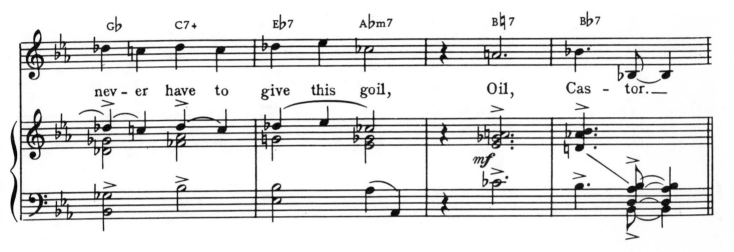

nev - er have to give this goil, Oil, Cas - tor.—

REFRAIN (Brightly)

I'm al - ways— a flop at — a top notch— af -

fair, I've still got— my health— so what do I care! —————

My best ring,— a - las is — a glass sol - i-

taire, I've still got — my health — so what do I

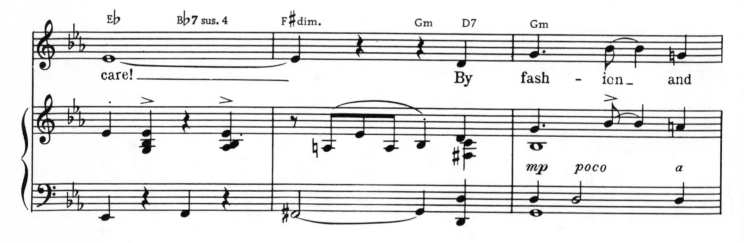

care! _____ By fash - ion — and

fopp' - ry — I'm nev - er — dis - cussed, At -

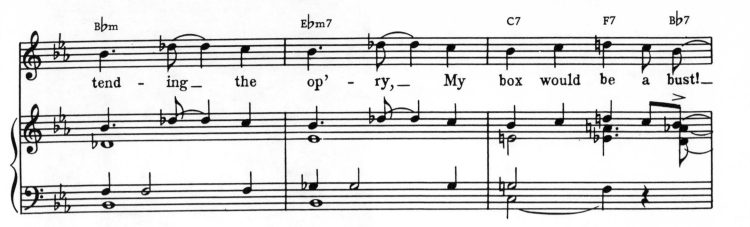

tend - ing _ the op' - ry, _ My box would be a bust! _

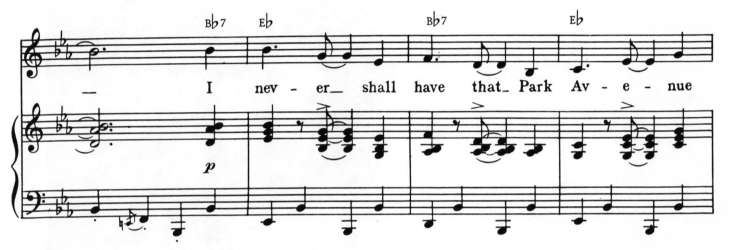

_ I nev - er _ shall have that _ Park Av - e - nue

air, _____ Well, I've still got _ my health _ so what do I

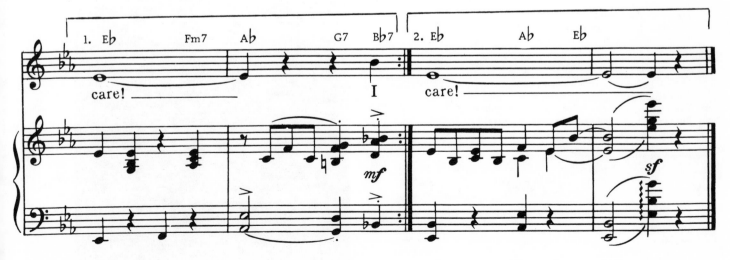

care! _____ I care! _____

I'VE STILL GOT MY HEALTH

REFRAIN 1

I'm always a flop at a top-notch affair,
But I've still got my health, so what do II care!
My best ring, alas, is a glass solitaire,
But I've still got my health, so what do I care!
By fashion and fopp'ry
I'm never discussed,
Attending the op'ry,
My box would be a bust!
When I give a tea, Lucius Beebe ain't there,
Well, I've still got my health, so what do I care!

VERSE 2

In spite of my Lux Movie skin
And Brewster body,
I've never joined the harem in
Scheherazade,
But, if so far, I've been a bust,
I'm stronger than the Bankers Trust
And you never have to give *this* one
Hunyadi.

REFRAIN 2

No rich Vanderbilt gives me gilt underwear,
But I've still got my health, so what do I care!
I've never been dined by refined L. B. Mayer,
But I've still got my health, so what do I care!
When Barrymore, he played
With his wife of yore,
The lead Missus B played,
But I played Barrymore,
She chased me a block for a lock of my hair,
Well, I've still got my health, so what do I care!

REFRAIN 3

I haven't the face of Her Grace, Ina Claire,
But I've still got my health, so what do I care!
I can't count my ribs, like His Nibs, Fred Astaire,
But I've still got my health, so what do I care!
Once I helped Jock Whitney
And as my reward,
I asked for a Jitney—
In other words, a Ford,
What I got from Jock was a sock, you know where,
Well, I've still got my health, so what do I care!

REFRAIN 4

When I'm in New York, I'm the Stork Club's despair,
But I've still got my health, so what do I care!
No radio chain wants my brain on the air,
But I've still got my health, so what do I care!
At school I was noted
For my lack of speed,
In fact I was voted
"Least likely to succeed,"
My wisecracks, I'm told are like old Camembert,
Well, I've still got my health, so what do I care!

VERSE 3

When Broadway first reviewed this wench,
The Press was catty,
They all agreed I'd even stench
In Cincinnati.
But, if I laid an awful egg,
I'm still as hot as Mayor Hague,
So in case you want to start a fire,
Wire Hattie.

REFRAIN 5

The hip that I shake doesn't make people stare,
But I've still got my health, so what do I care!
The sight of my props never stops thoroughfare,
But I've still got my health, so what do I care!
I knew I was slipping
At Minsky's one dawn,
When I started stripping,
They hollered "Put it on!"
Just once Billy Rose let me pose in the bare,
Well, I've still got my vitamins A, B, C, D,
E, F, G, H,
I
Still have my
Health.

Joan Carroll and Ethel Merman perform LET'S BE BUDDIES in PANAMA HATTIE (1940)

PANAMA HATTIE

Cole Porter's first show of the 1940s served as a good omen—another hit!

1. Ethel Merman, Rags Ragland, Frank Hyers, and Pat Harrington. 2. Ethel Merman. 3. Ann Sothern in the later MGM film version of PANAMA HATTIE. 4. Ethel Merman with Pat Harrington, Rags Ragland, and Frank Hyers.

5. Rags Ragland obviously approves of Ethel Merman's somewhat gaudy outfit. The costumes and sets were designed by Raoul Pene du Bois.

MAKE IT ANOTHER OLD FASHIONED, PLEASE

COLE PORTER

Since I went on the wag - on, I'm _____. cer - tain

drink is a maj - or crime, _____ For when you lay off the li -quor you

feel so much slick - er, Well, that is, most __ of the

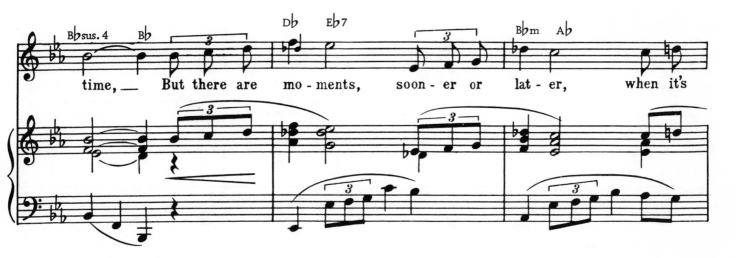

time, __ But there are mo - ments, soon - er or lat - er, when it's

tough, I got __ to say, not to say: "Wait - er! __

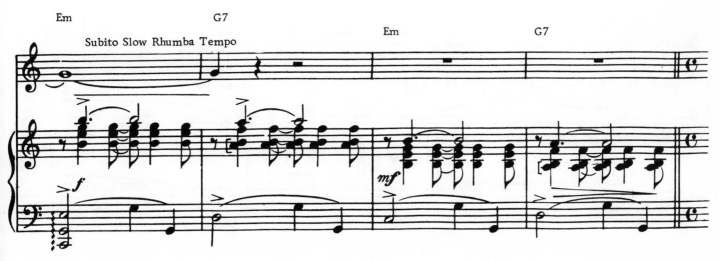

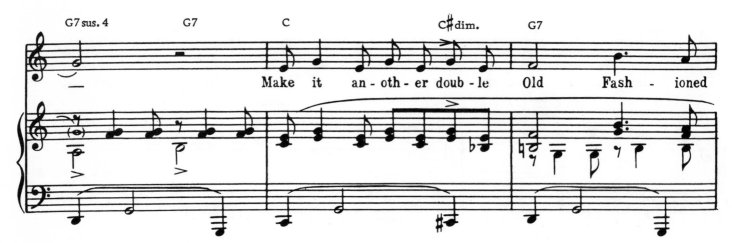

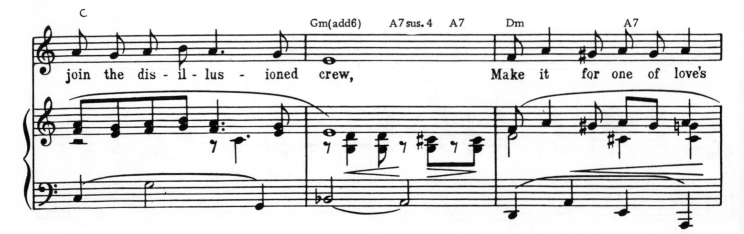

new,_____ ref - u - gees,_____ Once high in my cas - tle,

I reigned su - preme,_____ And Oh! what a cas - tle

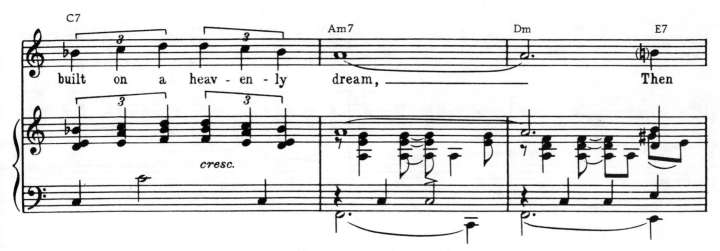

built on a heav - en - ly dream,_____ Then

quick as a light - ning flash, That cas - tle be - gan to crash, So

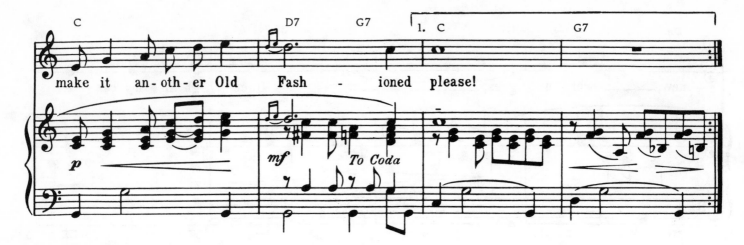

make it an-oth-er Old Fash - ioned please!

Final ending

please! _____ please! _____ Leave out the

Coda

cher-ry _____ Leave out the o - range! _____ Leave out the

bit - ters! ___ Just make it a straight rye! _____

Let's Face It

RUB YOUR LAMP

Vinton Freedley
presents

LET'S FACE IT

with Danny Kaye...
music + lyrics by Cole Porter
book by Dorothy + Herbert Fields
dances by Charles Walters
Book staged by Edgar MacGregor

A LITTLE RUMBA NUMBA
FARMING
EV'RYTHING I LOVE
YOU IRRITATE ME SO
RUB YOUR LAMP
ACE IN THE HOLE

CHAPPELL
& CO · INC·
RKO BUILDING
ROCKEFELLER
CENTER·N·Y·C
CHAPPELL
MADE IN U.S.A. & CO·LTD·LONDON

Produced by **VINTON FREEDLEY**

First performance: October 29, 1941 at the
Imperial Theatre, New York
playing for 547 performances

Music & Lyrics by **COLE PORTER**
Book by **HERBERT & DOROTHY FIELDS**

Staged by **EDGAR MacGREGOR**

The cast included:
Danny Kaye, Eve Arden, Benny Baker, Mary
Jane Walsh, Edith Meiser, Vivian Vance, Sunnie
O'Dea, Nanette Fabray, and Jack Williams

FARMING

COLE PORTER

Here's a bit o' news that's quite a shock-er, Prov-ing Moth-er Na-ture still has charm,

Quot-ing Mis-ter Chol-ly Knick-er-bock-er "Get in the swim and buy a farm,"

A-cres of al-fal-fa, fields of clo-ver Sud-den-ly en-chant our top"Who's who,"

So the mo-ment all this row is o-ver What say if we go hay-seed too,— For

REFRAIN (faster and brighter)

Farm - ing,— that's the fash - ion, Farm - ing,—

that's the pas-sion of our great ce-leb - ri-ties of to-day,—

Fan - nie Hurst is haul - in' logs, ___

Fan - nie Brice is call - in' hogs, ___ Gar - Bo - peep has led

_ her sheep all a - stray, ___ Hoe - ing ___

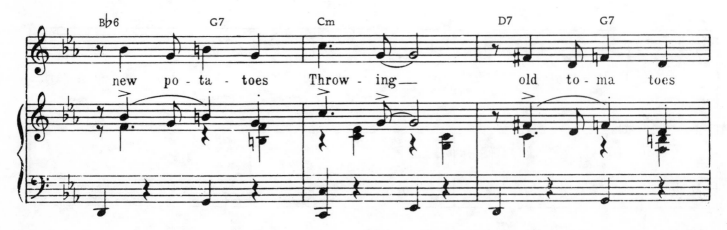

new po - ta - toes Throw - ing ___ old to - ma toes

Makes 'em feel more glam-our-ous and more gay, _____ They

tell me cows who are feel-ing milk-y All give cream when they're

milked by Will-kie, Farm-ing ___ is so charm-ing, they all

say. _____ say. _____

135

Jack Williams, Nanette Fabray, Danny Kaye, Sunnie O'Dea, and Benny Baker perform FARMING in LET'S FACE IT (1941)

REFRAIN 1

Farming, that's the fashion,
Farming, that the passion
Of our great celebrities of today.
Kit Cornell is shellin' peas,
Lady Mendl's climbin' trees,
Dear Mae West is at her best in the hay,
Stomping through the thickets,
Romping with the crickets,
Makes 'em feel more glamorous and more gay,
They tell me cows who are feeling milky
All give cream when they're milked by Willkie,
Farming is so charming, they all say.

REFRAIN 2

Farming, that's the fashion,
Farming, that's the passion
Of our great celebrities of today.
Monty Woolley, so I heard,
Has boll weevils in his beard,
Michael Strange has got the mange, will it stay?
Mussing up the clover,
Cussing when it's over,
Makes 'em feel more glamorous and more gay.
The natives think it's utterly utter
When Margie Hart starts churning her butter,
Farming is so charming, they all say.

REFRAIN 3

Farming, that's the fashion,
Farming, that's the passion
Of our great celebrities of today.
Fannie Hurst is haulin' logs,
Fannie Brice is feedin' hogs,
Garbo-Peep has led her sheep all astray,
Singing while they're rakin',
Bringing home the bacon,
Makes 'em feel more glamorous and more gay.
Miss Elsa Maxwell, so the folks tattle,
Got well-goosed while de-horning her cattle,
Farming is so charming, they all say.

REFRAIN 4

Farming that's the fashion,
Farming, that's the passion
Of our great celebrities of today.
Don't inquire of Georgie Raft
Why his cow has never calfed,
Georgia's bull is beautiful, but he's gay!
Seeing spring a-coming,
Being minus plumbing,
Makes 'em feel informal and dégagé.
When Cliff Odets found a new tomater
He ploughed under the Group Theaytre,
Farming is so charming, they all say.

REFRAIN 5

Farming, that's the fashion,
Farming, that's the passion,
Of our great celebrities of today.
Steinbeck's growing Grapes of Wrath,
Guy Lombardo, rumor hath,
Toots his horn and all the corn starts to sway,
Racing like the dickens,
Chasing after chickens,
Makes 'em feel more glamorous and more gay,
Liz Whitney has, on her bin of manure, a
Clip designed by the Duke of Verdura,
Farming is so charming, they all say.

(Among the discarded lines were the following:)

Farming, that's the fashion,
Farming, that's the passion
Of our great celebrities of today.
Digging in his fertile glen,
Goldwyn dug up Anna Sten,
Fred Astaire has raised a hare and its gray.
Clowning in their mittens,
Drowning extra kittens,
Makes 'em feel more glamorous and more gay.
Paul Whiteman, while he was puttin' up jelly,
Ate so much he recovered his belly,
Farming is so charming, they all say.

Farming, that's the fashion,
Farming, that's the passion,
Of our great celebrities of today
Missus Henry Morganthau
Looks so chic behind a plow,
Mrs. Hearst is at her worst on a dray.
Tearing after possum,
Wearing just a blossom,
Makes 'em feel more glamorous and more gay,
Why Orson Welles, that wonderful actor,
Has Del Rio driving a tractor.
Farming is so charming, they all say.

Farming, that's the fashion,
Farming, that's the passion,
Of our great celebrities of today.
Just to keep her roosters keen,
Dietrich that great movie queen,
Lifts her leg and lays an egg, what a lay.
Going after rabbits,
Knowing all their habits,
Makes 'em feel more glamorous and more gay.
So Harpo Marx, in a moment of folly,
Had his barn repainted by Dali.
Farming is so charming, they all say.

Farming, that's the fashion,
Farming, that's the passion,
Of our great celebrities of today.
Lynn Fontanne is brandin' steer,
Sophie Tucker, so I hear,
Rides en masse upon an ass, hip-hooray.
Hoeing new potatoes,
Throwing all tomatoes,
Makes 'em feel more glamorous and more gay.
So Clifton Webb has parked his Ma, Mabel,
"Way Down East" in a broken-down stable,
Farming is so charming, they all say.

Danny Kaye and Cole Porter confer during a rehearsal of LET'S FACE IT

LET'S NOT TALK ABOUT LOVE

COLE PORTER

SHE

Tempo di Barcarolle

lax for one mo-ment, my Jer-ry,___ Come out of your dark mon-as-te-ry___ While

Ve-nus is beam-ing a-bove,___ Dar-ling, let's talk a-bout love.___ My

HE

Valse Tempo

bud-dies all tell me se-lec-tees___ Are ex-pect-ed by

la - dies to neck - tease,_____ I could talk a - bout love and why

not? But be - lieve me, it would - n't be so hot, So let's

REFRAIN (Lightly and rhytmically)

talk a - bout frogs, Let's talk a - bout toads, Let's try to solve the rid - dle why

chick - ens cross roads, Let's talk a - bout games, Let's talk a - bout sports, Let's

have a big de - bate a - bout la - dies in shorts, Let's check on the ve - ra - ci - ty of

Bar - ry - more's bi - ba - ci - ty And why his drink ca - pa - ci - ty should get so much pub - la - ci - ty, Let's

e - ven have a hud - dle o - ver Ha' - vard U - ni - va - si - ty, But let's not talk a - bout

love Let's wish him good luck, Let's wish him more pow'r That Fi - o - rel - la fel - la, my

favorite flow'r Let's curse the Old Guard and Ham-il-ton Fish, For-

give me, dear if Fish is your fav-or-ite dish, Let's write a tune that's play-a-ble, a

dit-ty swing-and-sway-a-ble, Or say what ev-er's say-a-ble a-bout the Tow'r of Ba-a-bel, Let's

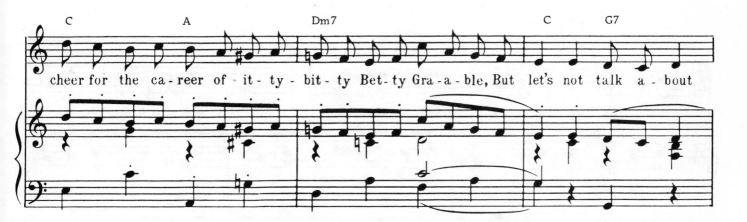

cheer for the ca-reer of it-ty bit-ty Bet-ty Gra-a-ble, But let's not talk a-bout

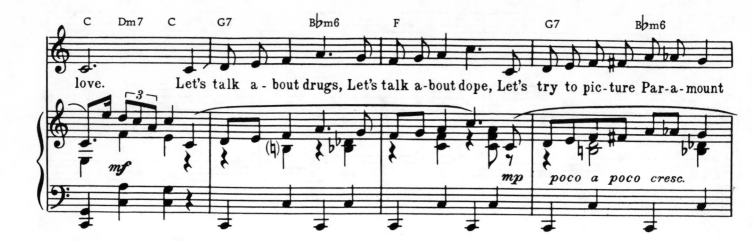

love. Let's talk a - bout drugs, Let's talk a-bout dope, Let's try to pic-ture Par-a-mount

mi - nus Bob Hope, Let's start a new dance, Let's try a new step, Or in-

ves - ti-gate the cause of Mis-sus Roos- e -velt's pep, Why not dis-cuss, my dee-a-rie, The

life of Wal-lace Bee-a - ry, Or bring a jer-o-bo-am on And write a drunk-en po-em on Ti-

mid - i - ty, stu-pid - i - ty, sol - id - i - ty, fri-gid - i - ty, a - vid - i - ty, tur-bid - i - ty, Man-

hat-tan and vi-cid - i - ty, Fa - tal - i - ty, mo-ral - i - ty, le - gal - i - ty, fi - nal - i - ty, Neu-

tral - i - ty, re - al - i - ty or south-ern hos-pi-tal - i - ty, Pom - pos - i - ty, ver-bos - i - ty, I'm

los-ing my ve-loc - i - ty, But let's not talk a - bout love. Let's love.

LET'S NOT TALK ABOUT LOVE

REFRAIN 2

Let's talk about frogs, let's talk about toads,
Let's try to solve the riddle why chickens
   cross roads,
Let's talk about games, let's talk about sports,
Let's have a big debate about ladies in shorts,
Let's question the synonymy of freedom
   and autonomy,
Let's delve into astronomy, political economy,
Or if you're feeling biblical, the book
   of Deuteronomy,
But let's not talk about love.
Let's ride the New Deal, like Senator Glass,
Let's telephone to Ickes and order more gas,
Let's curse the Old Guard and Hamilton Fish,
Forgive me, dear, if Fish is your favorite dish,
Let's heap some hot profanities on Hitler's
   inhumanities,
Let's argue if insanity's the cause of
   his inanities,
Let's weigh the Shubert Follies with The Ear-rl
   Carroll Vanities,
But let's not talk about love.
Let's talk about drugs, let's talk about dope,
Let's try to picture Paramount minus Bob Hope,
Let's start a new dance, let's try a new step,
Or investigate the cause of Missus Roosevelt's pep,
Why not discus, my dee-arie,
The life of Wallace Bee-ery
Or bring a jeroboam on
And write a drunken poem on
Astrology, mythology,
Geology, philology,
Pathology, psychology,
Electro-physiology,
Spermology, phrenology,
I owe you an apology
But let's not talk about love.

REFRAIN 3

Let's speak of Lamarr, the Hedy so fair,
Why does she let Joan Bennett wear all
   her old hair?
If you know Garbo, then tell me this news,
Is it a fact the Navy's launched all
   her old shoes?
Let's check on the veracity of Barrymore's
   bibacity
And why his drink capacity should get so
   much publacity,
Let's even have a huddle over Ha'vard
   Univassity,
But let's not talk about love.
Let's wish him good luck, let's wish him
   more pow'r,
That Fiorella fella, my favorite flow'r,
Let's get some champagne from over
   the seas,
And drink to Sammy Goldwyn,
Include me out please.
Let's write a tune that's playable,
   a ditty swing-and-swayable
Or say whatever's sayable, about the
   Tow'r of Ba-abel,
Let's cheer for the career of itty-bitty
   Betty Gra-abel,
But let's not talk about love.
In case you play cards, I've got some
   right here
So how about a game o' gin-rummy, my dear?
Or if you feel warm and bathin's your whim,
Let's get in the all-together and
   enjoy a short swim,
No honey, Ah suspect you all
Of bein' intellectual
And so, instead of gushin' on,
Let's have a big discussion on
Timidity, stupidity, solidity, frigidity,
Avidity, turbidity, Manhattan, and viscidity,
Fatality, morality, legality, finality,
Neutrality, reality, or Southern hospitality,
Pomposity, verbosity,
You're losing your velocity
But let's not talk about love.

144

LET'S FACE IT

Another hit for Cole Porter in 1941 as LET'S FACE IT took Broadway by storm. The superb cast assembled for this show comprised such stars as (top photo, left to right) Eve Arden, Danny Kaye, Edith Meiser, Benny Baker, Jack Williams and Vivian Vance. Below: The same stars, different pose. Even the outbreak of World War II December 7, 1941 didn't stop LET'S FACE IT from playing a total of 547 performances, a long run for those days!

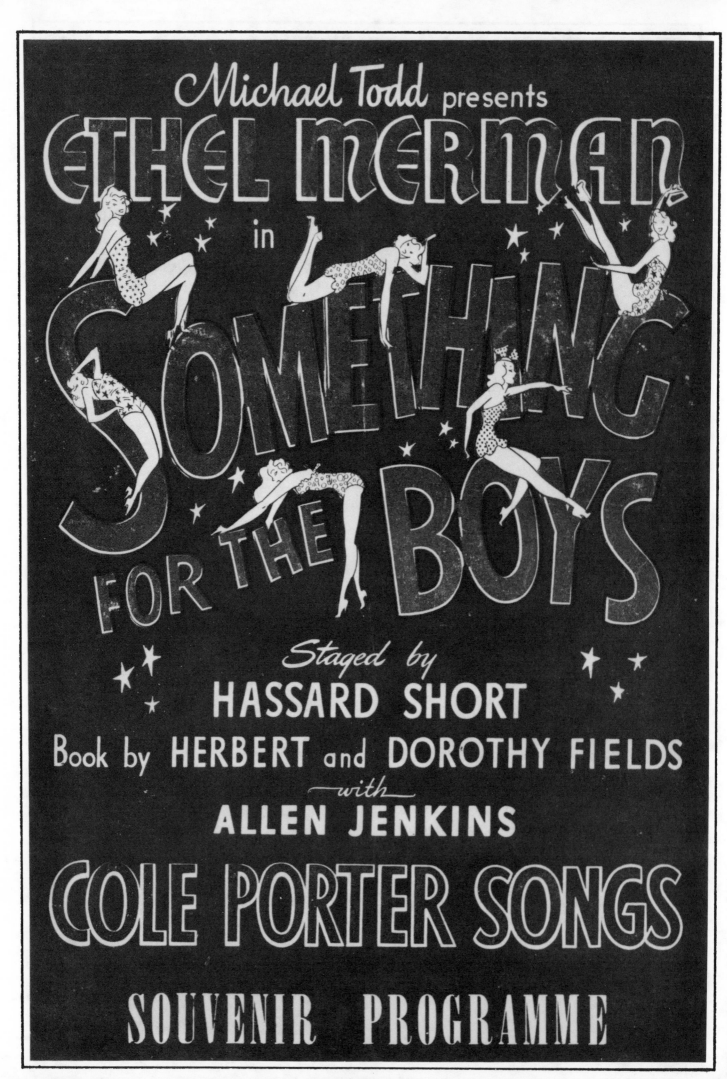

Michael Todd presents

ETHEL MERMAN

in

SOMETHING

for the BOYS

Staged by
HASSARD SHORT

Book by HERBERT and DOROTHY FIELDS
with
ALLEN JENKINS

COLE PORTER SONGS

SOUVENIR PROGRAMME

Something For The Boys

Produced by **MICHAEL TODD**

First performance: January 7, 1943 at the
Alvin Theatre, New York
playing for 422 performances

Music & Lyrics by **COLE PORTER**
Book by **HERBERT & DOROTHY FIELDS**

Staged by **HASSARD SHORT**
Settings by **HOWARD BAY**
Costumes by **BILLY LIVINGSTON**
Choreography by **JACK COLE**
Musical Direction by **WILLIAM PARSON**

The cast included:
Ethel Merman, Paula Laurence, Bill Johnson,
Betty Garrett, Betty Bruce, and Allen Jenkins

THE LEADER OF A BIG TIME BAND

COLE PORTER

If a girl in an-y sec-tor, Makes you feel like the pup-py called Hec-tor, And you're

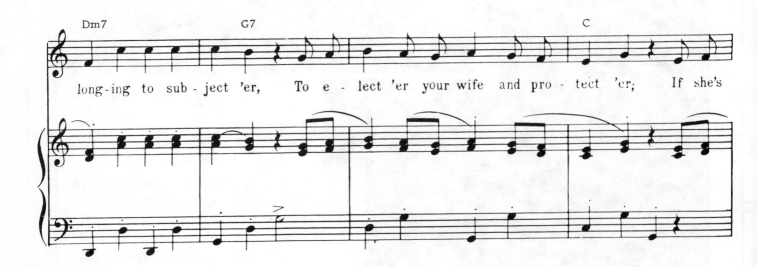

long-ing to sub-ject 'er, To e-lect 'er your wife and pro-tect 'er; If she's

just as sweet as nec-tar, But of your job she's no re-spect-er, Be-come a

top band di-rect-or And you nev-er, nev-er will miss.

REFRAIN

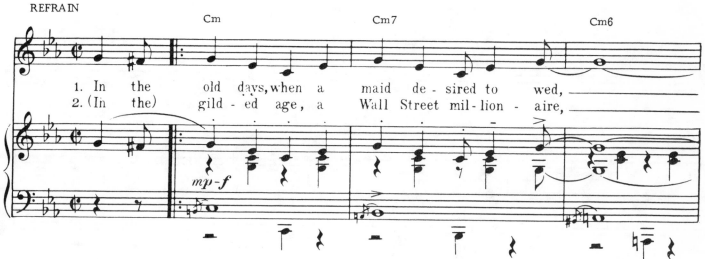

1. In the old days, when a maid de-sired to wed, ____
2. (In the) gild-ed age, a Wall Street mil-lion-aire, ____

— An-y beau who had the dough could go a-head, ____
— Was the an-swer to a work-ing maid-en's prayer, ____

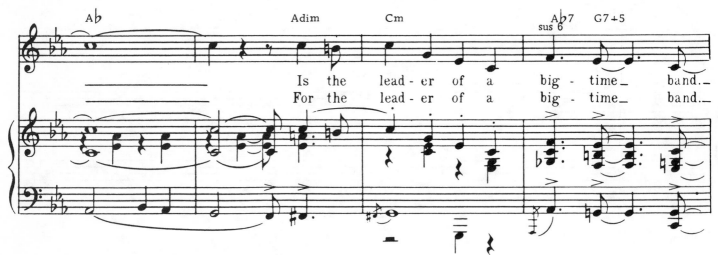

Dear Mis - sus   Van - der - bilt —   Bumps her - self   out;—
Rum - rid - den   de - bu - tramps   Near - ly come   to! —

So   if   thee would like   to   be   in great de - mand,—
'Cause there's   noth - ing, when you're   out, like be - ing   fanned_

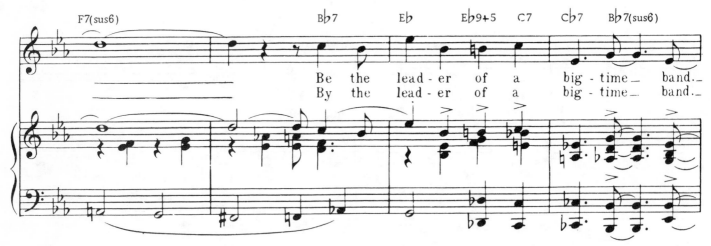

Be   the   lead - er   of   a   big - time_   band.
By   the   lead - er   of   a   big - time_   band._

2. In   the

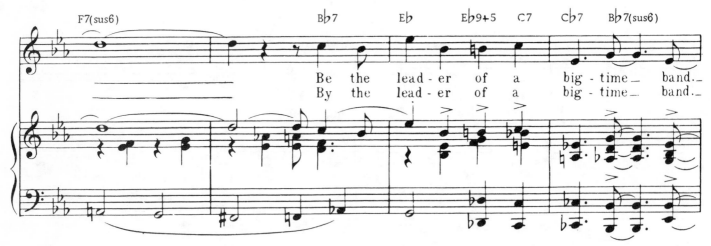

152

THE LEADER OF A BIG TIME BAND
Complete Version

REFRAIN 1

In the old days, when a maid desired to wed,
Any man who'd foot the bill could fill the bed,
But today the lad who's sure to win her hand
Is the leader of a big-time band.
Even gals who go for wrestlers quit 'em quick
When they meet some guy who sings and swings a stick,
For of late the only date they long to land
Is the leader of a big-time band.
When they hear Harry James
Make with the lips
The most Colonial Dames
Fracture their hips,
(So if Thee would like to be in great demand,
Be the leader of a big-time band.)

REFRAIN 2

In the gilded age, a Wall Street millionaire
Was the answer to a working maiden's prayer,
But today she'd chuck that yearly fifty grand
For the leader of a big-time band.
In the days when Casanova was the tops
All his rivals with the femmes were famous flops,
But today's who got that extra monkey gland?
Why, the leader of a big-time band.
When Goodman, champ of champs,
Goes blowin' blue,
Rum-ridden debutramps
Nearly come to,
'Cause there's nothing, when you're out,
    like being fanned
By the leader of a big-time band.

REFRAIN 3

In the days when old King Louie held the scene,
Any Jock who had the Jack could play the Queen,
But today who'd come and play that baby grand?
Why, the leader of a big-time band.
When, in Venice, Georgia Sand with Chopin romped,
Her libido had the Lido simply swamped,
But today who would be buried in the sand?
Why, the leader of a big-time band.
When Dorsey starts to tilt
That horn about,
Dear Missus Vanderbilt
Bumps herself out,
So, if, say, you still can play a one-night stand,
Be the leader of a big-time band.

REFRAIN 4

When in Reno ladies we know used to clown,
All the chaps who wore the shaps could wear 'em down,
But today the only rider they demand
Is the leader of a big-time band,
When Salome got John the B. and by the head,
It appears he wasn't kosher in da bed.
But today who'd be the goy she'd like to land?
Why, the leader of a big-time band.
When Cugat comes to tea
With Gypsy Rose,
She gets so het-up, she
Puts on her cloe's,
And she only turns one cheek while being scanned
By the leader of a big-time, jig-time,
    dig a-dig-time band.

Ethel Merman with Bill Johnson (above) and Allen Jenkins (below)

153

SOMETHING FOR THE BOYS
1. The company. 2. SOMETHING FOR THE BOYS premiered on an evening unique in the history of Broadway. January 7, 1943 the O.P.A. decreed no private automobiles could be driven to places of entertainment. Needless to point out, the taxi industry experienced a boon in business as this photo of the arrivals for opening night attests. Co-incidentally, Ethel Merman was playing the Alvin Theatre for the first time since her initial Broadway triumph in GIRL CRAZY some 13 years previously. 3. Ethel Merman.

Something To Shout About

A COLUMBIA PICTURES Film

Produced by **GREGORY RATOFF**

Released in February, 1943

Music & Lyrics by **COLE PORTER**
Screenplay by **LOU BRESLOW & EDWARD ELISCU**

Directed by **GREGORY RATOFF**

The cast included:
Don Ameche, Janet Blair, William Gaxton,
Jack Oakie, Hazel Scott, Cobina Wright Jr.,
and Veda Ann Borg

YOU'D BE SO NICE TO COME HOME TO

COLE PORTER

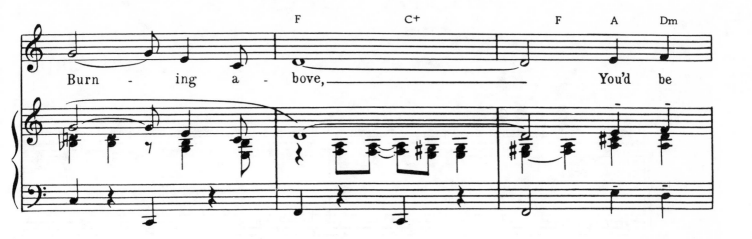

Burn - ing a - bove, _____ You'd be

so nice, You'd be par - a - dise to come

1. home to _____ and love. _____ You'd be

2. home to _____ and love. _____

HASTA LUEGO

COLE PORTER

Lively Rumba tempo

1. In a small can - tee - na,— on an is - land far,
2. (Se - no - ri - ta) Lee - na,— had no love af - fairs,
3. (Once they'd mar - ried,) Lee - na,— and her rich old guy,

Se - no - ri - ta Lee - na,— Sang a song to a hot gui - tar,—
'Til from Pas - a - de - na — Came the last of the mil - lion-aires_
Moved to Pas - a - de - na — Where the best peo-ple go to die,—

All the ding - dong dan - dies,_ Used to gath - er a -
Af - ter glimps - ing Lee - na,_ This ty - coon of fi -
But when she'd col - lect - ed,_ All his cop - per pre -

bout, When the love - ly Lee - na,_ La di -
nance Felt so full of life, he _ Wired his
ferred, Back to her can - tee - na,_ Love - ly

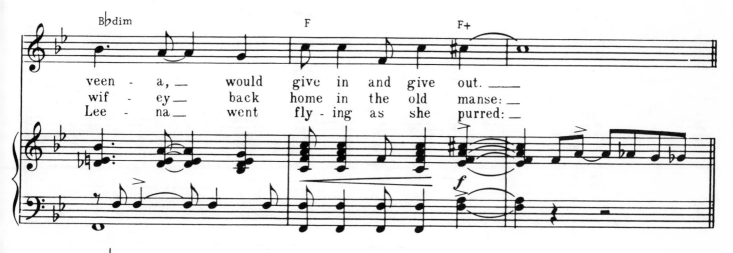

veen - a, _ would give in and give out. ____
wif - ey _ back home in the old manse: _
Lee - na _ went fly - ing as she purred: _

REFRAIN

Has - ta _____ lu - e - go, _____

Too bad _____ we must part, _____

Has - ta _____ lu - e - go _____ And here's

1.

mooch - a _____ good luck, sweet-heart. _____ Se - no - ri - ta
Once they'd mar - ried,

2.

mooch - a _____ good luck, sweet-heart. _____

Mexican Hayride

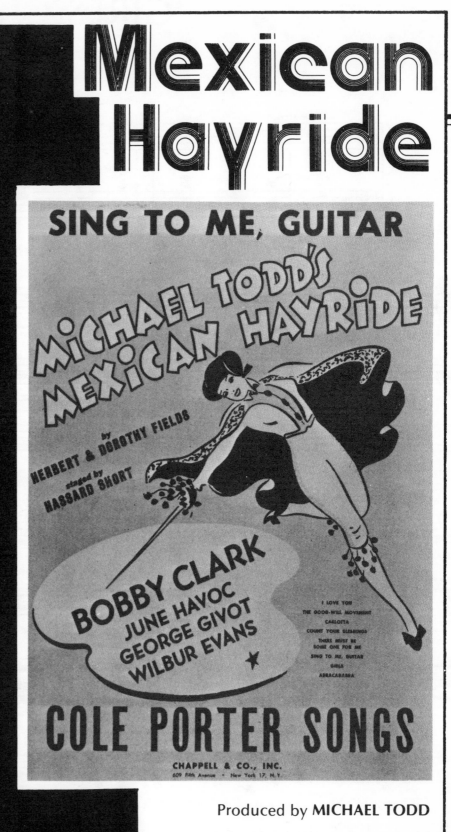

Produced by **MICHAEL TODD**

First performance: January 28, 1944 at the Winter Garden Theatre, New York playing for 481 performances

Music & Lyrics by **COLE PORTER**
Book by **HERBERT & DOROTHY FIELDS**

Staged & Lighted by **HASSARD SHORT**

The cast included:
Bobby Clark, June Havoc, George Givot, Wilbur Evans, Luba Malina, Corinna Mura, Paul Haakon and Eric Schepard

GIRLS

COLE PORTER

He: An old gyp - sy proph - e - sied when I was three.__ Girls: And what did she tell

__ our lit - tle star?_____ He: That, one day, a la - dy kil - ler

I would be.__ Girls: And now, dear, you cer - tain - ly are._____ He: Yes,

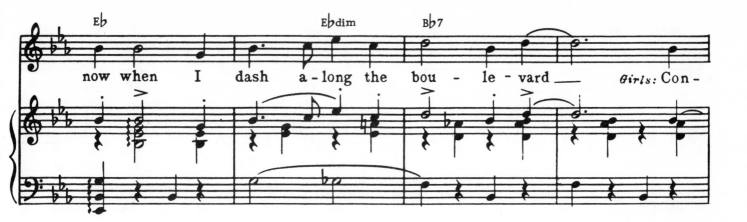

now when I dash a-long the bou - le - vard ___ *Girls:* Con-

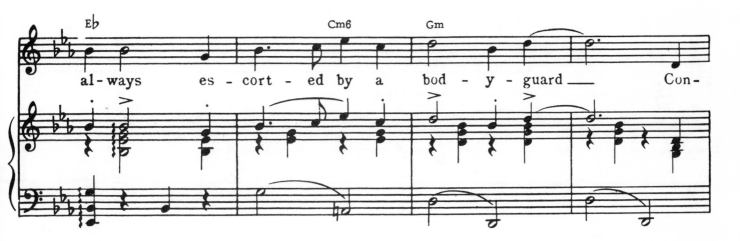

tin - ue, oh, man we love! ___ *He:* I'm

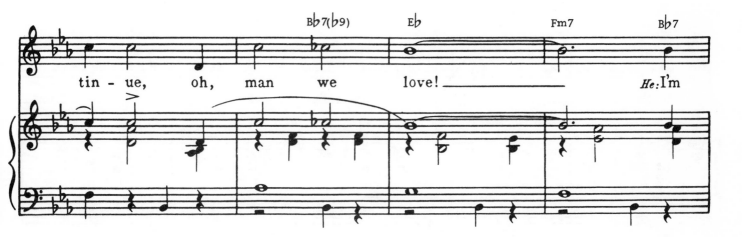

al-ways es - cort - ed by a bod - y - guard ___ Con-

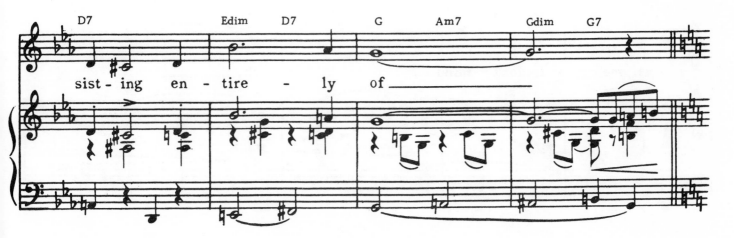

sist - ing en - tire - ly of ___

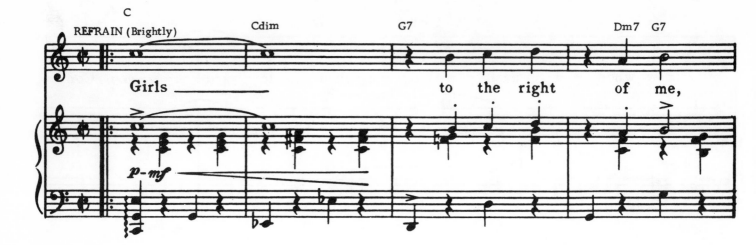

what a rogue am I, So _____

much in vogue am I. Sim - ply smoth __ ered in

kiss - es and curls __ by the girls, girls, girls, girls,

1. girls. _____

2. girls. _____

MEXICAN HAYRIDE
1. Bobby Clark. 2. Hassard Short, who staged MEXICAN HAYRIDE and many other Cole Porter shows. 3. Bobby Clark (alias Joe Bascom, alias Humphrey Fish) and June Havoc as the bullfighter known as Montana.

BOB GOLBY

I LOVE YOU

COLE PORTER

las, just an am - a - teur am I _____ And so I'll

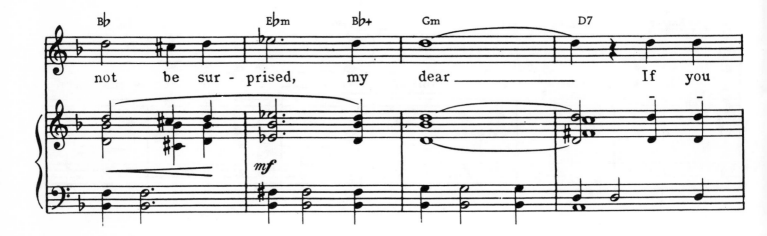

not be sur - prised, my dear _____ If you

smile and po - lite - ly pass it by _____ When this, my

first_ love song, you hear_____

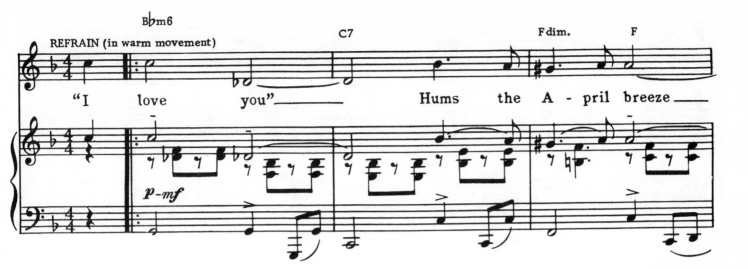

171

more she sees daf - fo - dils

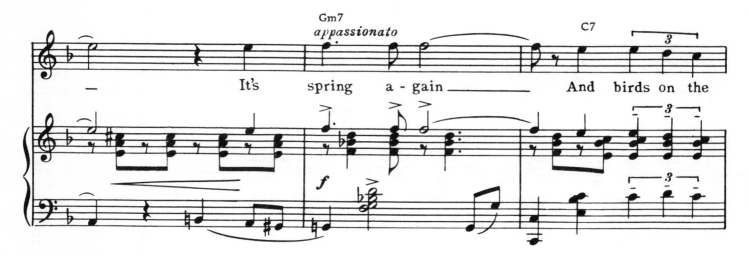

It's spring a - gain And birds on the

wing a - gain start to sing a - gain

The old mel - o - die "I

love you" ___ That's the song of songs, ___ And it

all be-longs to you and me. ___ I

me ___ And it all be - longs ___ to you and

me. ___

Out Of This World

Cherry Pies Ought To Be You

Produced by **SAINT SUBBER & LEMUEL AYRES**

First performance: December 21, 1950 at the
New Century Theatre, New York
playing for 157 performances

Music & Lyrics by **COLE PORTER**
Book by **DWIGHT TAYLOR & REGINALD LAWRENCE**

Entire production staged by **AGNES deMILLE**
Choreography by **HANYA HOLM**
Settings & Costumes by **LEMUEL AYRES**
Musical Direction by **PEMBROKE DAVENPORT**

The cast included:
Charlotte Greenwood, William Eythe, Priscilla
Gillette, William Redfield, Barbara Ashley, Janet
Collins, George Jongeyans (Gaynes), Ray Harrison,
and David Burns

CHERRY PIES OUGHT TO BE YOU

COLE PORTER

He: Oh, by Jove and by Je - ho - vah, you have set my heart a - flame. She: And to you, young Ca - sa - no - va, my re -

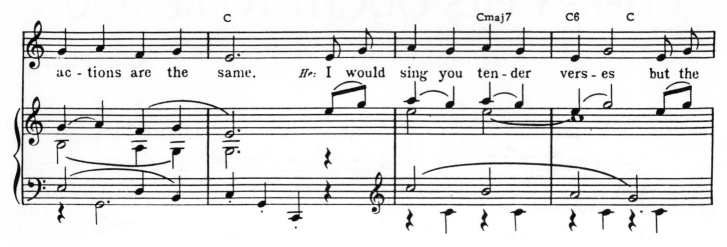

ac - tions are the same. *He:* I would sing you ten - der vers - es but the

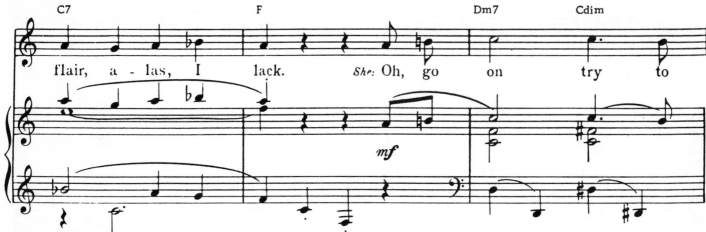

flair, a - las, I lack. *She:* Oh, go on try to

ver - si - fy and I'll ver - si - fy back.

REFRAIN (Graceful, steady fox-trot tempo)

She: Au - tumn skies _____ ought to be

He: Cher - ry pies _____ ought to be you,

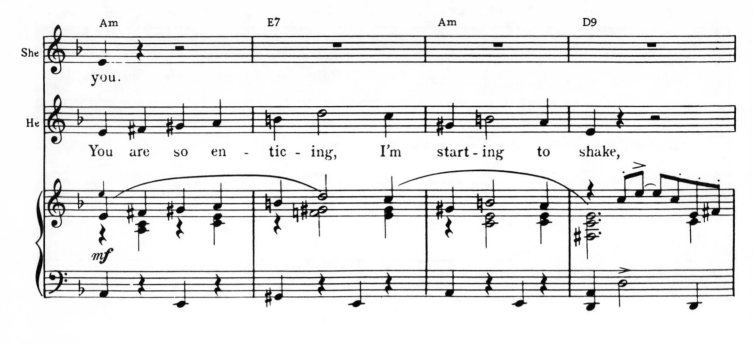

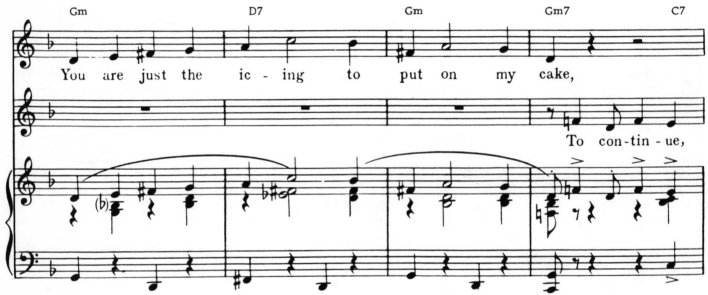

CHERRY PIES OUGHT TO BE YOU
Complete Version

REFRAIN 1

Mercury: Cherry pies ought to be you,
Chloe: Autumn skies ought to be you,
Mercury: Mister Pulitzer's prize ought to be you,
Chloe: Romeo in disguise ought to be you,
Mercury: Columbine ought to be you,
Chloe: Sparkling wine ought to be you,
Mercury: All of Beethoven's nine ought to be you,
Chloe: Ev'ry Will Shakespeare line ought to be you.
Mercury: You are so enticing, I'm starting to shake,
Chloe: You are just the icing to put on my cake,
Mercury: To continue,
      Whistler's ma ought to be you,
Chloe: Elliot's pa ought to be you,
Mercury: Ev'rything hip-hoorah ought to be you.
Chloe: French perfumes ought to be you,
Mercury: Texas booms ought to be you,
Chloe: Early Egyptian tombs ought to be you,
Mercury: Super Chief drawing rooms ought to be you,
Chloe: Hot Don Juan ought to be you,
Mercury: Yasmin Khan ought to be you,
Chloe: Cupid with nothing on ought to be you,
Mercury: Leda without her swan ought to be you.
Chloe: You may come a cropper, you're losing your breath,
Mercury: Were I not so proper, I'd squeeze you to death,
Chloe: To continue,
      Cary's chin ought to be you,
Mercury: Hepburn's grin ought to be you,
Chloe: Ev'rything sure to win ought to be you.
Mercury: Ought to be you,
Chloe: Ought to be you,
Mercury: Ought to be you,
Chloe: Ought to be you,
Mercury: Ought to be you,
Chloe: Ought to be you,
Mercury: Ought to be you,
Both: Ought to be
      You!

REFRAIN 2

Chloe: 'rabian nights ought to be you,
Mercury: Brooklyn Heights ought to be you,
Chloe: Joe Di Maggio in lights ought to be you,
Mercury: Garbo in Grable's tights ought to be you,
Chloe: Bergen's doll ought to be you,
Mercury: Parsons Loll ought to be you,
Chloe: India's Taj Mahal ought to be you,
Mercury: Fibber Magee's pet moll ought to be you.
Chloe: You have so much talent, you should be in shows,
Mercury: Were I not so gallant, I'd rip off your clo'es,
Chloe: To continue,
      Heaven's blue ought to be you,
Mercury: Heaven too ought to be you,
Chloe: Ev'rything super-do ought to be you.
Mercury: Ought to be you,
Chloe: Ought to be you,
Mercury: Ought to be you,
Chloe: Ought to be you,
Mercury: Ought to be you,
Chloe: Ought to be you,
Mercury: Ought to be you,
Both: Ought to be
      You!

REFRAIN 3

Mercury: Asphodels ought to be you,
Chloe: Orson Welles ought to be you,
Mercury: Ankles like Kit Cornell's ought to be you,
Chloe: Towels from Ritz hotels ought to be you,
Mercury: Sweet Snow White ought to be you,
Chloe: Ambrose Light ought to be you,
Mercury: Eleanor, wrong or right, ought to be you,
Chloe: Erroll Flynn, loose or tight, ought to be you.
Mercury: You are so exciting, I can't even laugh,
Chloe: If you're fond of biting, I'll bite you in half,
Mercury: To continue,
      Truman's Bess ought to be you,
Chloe: His success ought to be you,
Mercury: All except Truman's press ought to be you,
Chloe: Ought to be you,
Mercury: Ought to be you,
Chloe: Ought to be you,
Mercury: Ought to be you,
Chloe: Ought to be you,
Mercury: Ought to be you,
Chloe: Ought to be you,
Both: Ought to be
      You!

REPRISE 1

Niki: Shooting pains ought to be you,
Juno: Addled brains ought to be you,
Niki: Florida, when it rains, ought to be you,
Juno: Pinchers in subway trains ought to be you,
Niki: Withered grass ought to be you,
Juno: Lethal gas ought to be you,
Niki: Sour old applesass ought to be you,
Juno: Gabby old Balaam's ass ought to be you,
Niki: You, you look so fearful,
      You give me de joiks,
Juno: Kid, if you're not keerful,
      I'll give you de woiks,
Niki: To continue,
      Horse-meat steak ought to be you,
Juno: Pickled snake ought to be you,
Niki: Ev'rything I can't take ought to be you,
Juno: Ought to be you,
Niki: Ought to be you,
Juno: Ought to be you,
Niki: Ought to be you,
Juno: Ought to be you,
Niki: Ought to be you,
Juno: Ought to be you,
Both: Ought to be
      You!

REPRISE 2

Niki: Corn that's tough ought to be you,
Juno: In the rough ought to be you,
Niki: Ev'ry old powder puff ought to be you,
Juno: Ev'rything not enough ought to be you,
Niki: No one's bride ought to be you,
Juno: No one's pride ought to be you,
Niki: Just an old chicken fried ought to be you,
Juno: Cyanide, on the side, ought to be you,
Niki: That's darndest get-up
      That I've seen in years.
Juno: Kid, if you don't shet up,
      I'll pull off your ears.
Niki: To continue,
      No one's girl ought to be you,
Juno: Milton Berle ought to be you,
Niki: Salad with castor erl ought to be you,

Charlotte Greenwood does her famous high kick

Playbill for OUT OF THIS WORLD which opened Dec. 21, 1950 starring Charlotte Greenwood

Fred Fehl

FROM THIS MOMENT ON

COLE PORTER

Moderately slow

Now that we are close, no more nights mor - ose,

Now that we are one, the be - guine has just be - gun.

Now that we're side by side, the fu - ture looks so

gay, Now we are al - i - bi ed when we

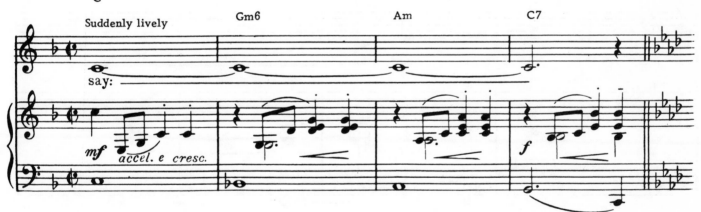

say:

From this mo - ment on,

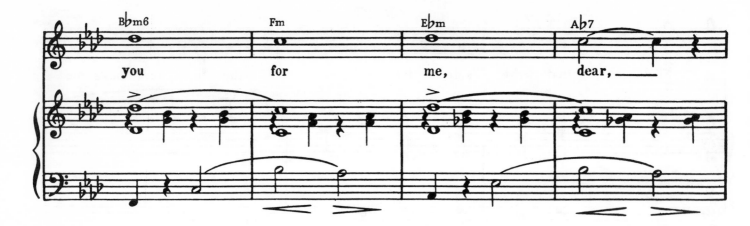

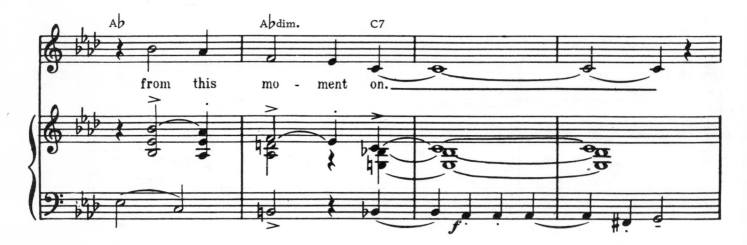

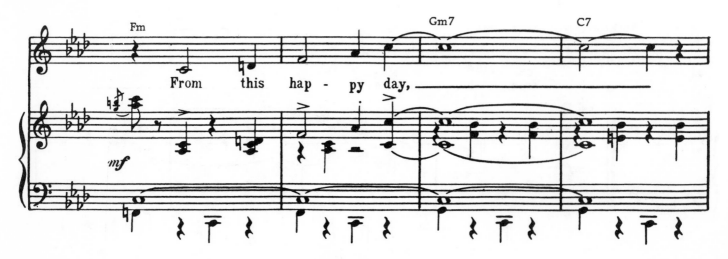

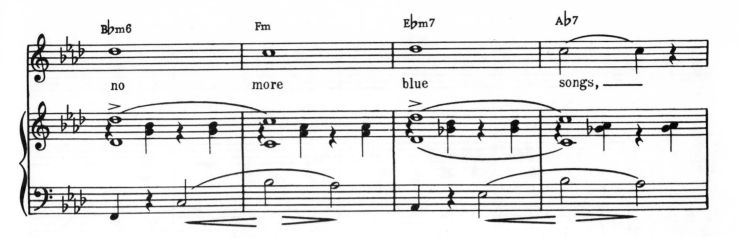

no more blue songs, ____

on - ly ____ whoop - dee - doo songs, ____

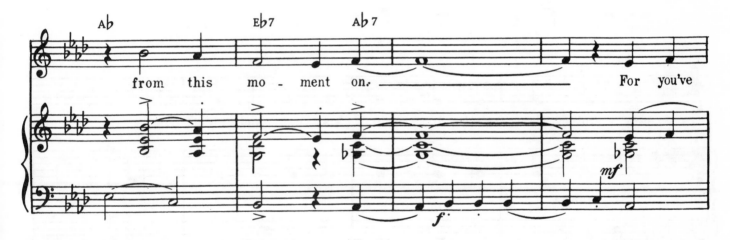

from this mo - ment on. ____ For you've

got the love ____ I need so much, ____

Got the skin — I love to touch, —

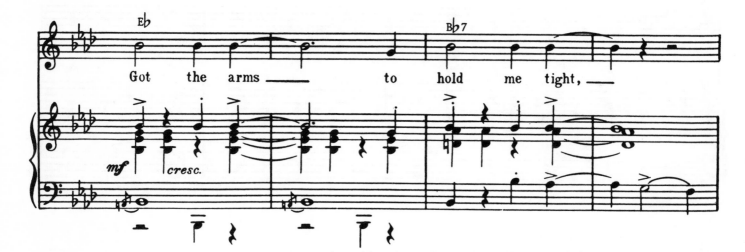

Got the arms — to hold me tight, —

mf *cresc.*

Got the sweet lips — to kiss me good - night, —

p subito

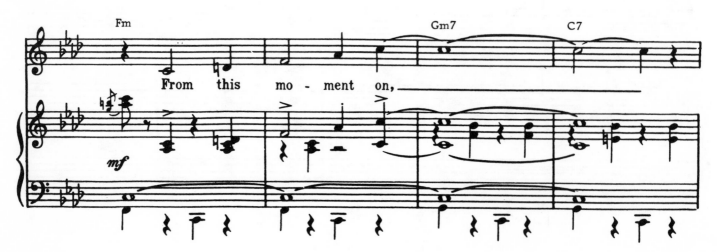

From this mo - ment on, —

mf

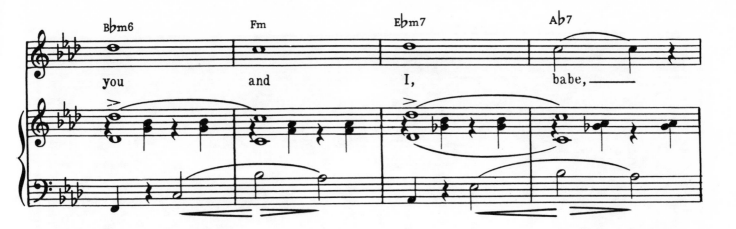

A beaming Cole Porter on a Hollywood set during the filming of "Kiss Me, Kate" in 1953

Can-Can

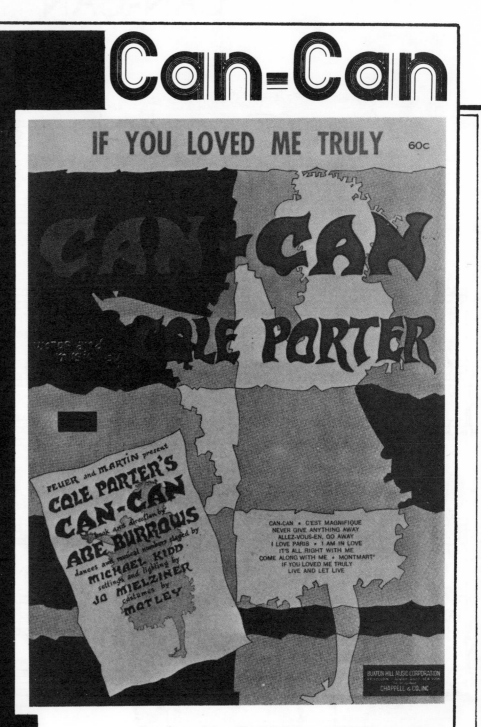

Produced by **CY FEUER & ERNEST MARTIN**

First performance: May 7, 1953 at the
Sam S. Shubert Theatre, New York
playing for 892 performances

Music & Lyrics by **COLE PORTER**
Book by **ABE BURROWS**

Directed by **ABE BURROWS**
Dances & Musical Numbers staged by **MICHAEL KIDD**
Settings & Lighting by **JO MIELZINER**
Costumes by **MOTLEY**
Musical Direction by **MILTON ROSENSTOCK**

The cast included:
Lilo, Peter Cookson, Hans Conreid, Gwen
Verdon, and Erik Rhodes

CAN-CAN

COLE PORTER

Lively Fox-Trot tempo

Ev - 'ry - bod - y,   chic   or   shod - dy,

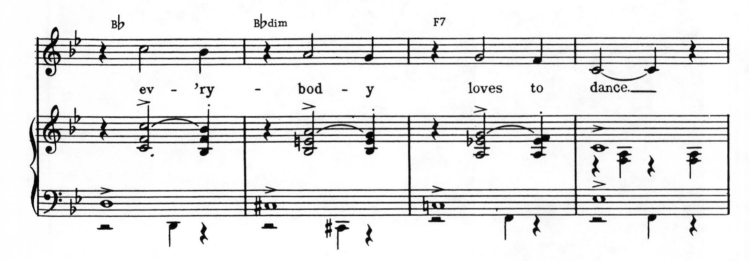

ev - 'ry - bod - y   loves   to   dance.___

Since that   big   dance,   in - fra - dig   dance,

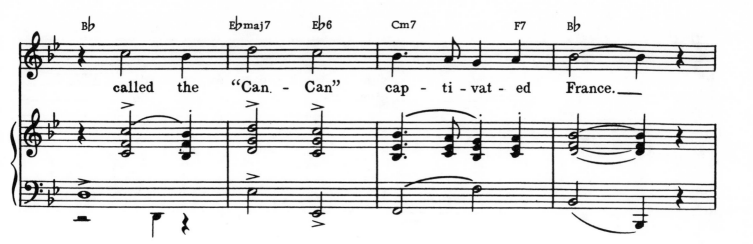

called the "Can. - Can" cap - ti -vat - ed France.____

Why does it kill ev - 'ry care?_____

Why is it done ev - 'ry - where?_____

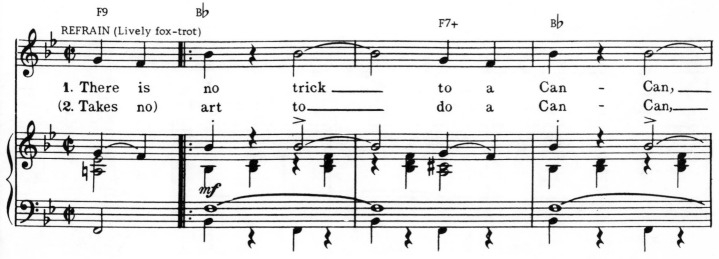

REFRAIN (Lively fox-trot)

1. There is no trick____ to a Can - Can,____
(2. Takes no) art to____ do a Can - Can,____

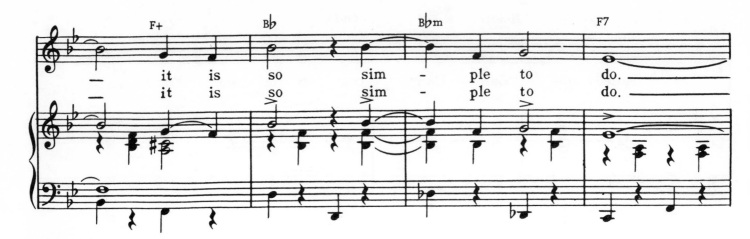

it is so sim - ple to do. ____
it is so sim - ple to do. ____

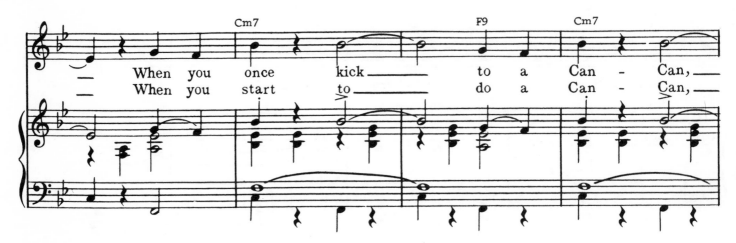

When you once kick ____ to a Can - Can, ____
When you start to ____ do a Can - Can, ____

'twill be so eas - y for you. ____
'twill be so eas' - y for you. ____

If a la - dy ____ in I - ran can, ____
If a slow Mo - ham - med - an can, ____

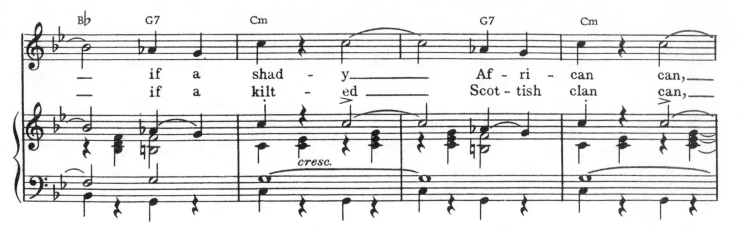

if a shad - y_____ Af - ri - can can,_____
if a kilt - ed _____ Scot - tish clan can,_____

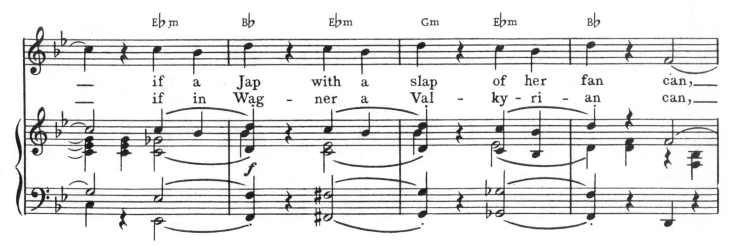

if a Jap with a slap of her fan can,_____
if in Wag - ner a Val - ky - ri - an can,_____

Ba - by, you can Can - Can too._____
Ba - by, you can Can - Can too._____

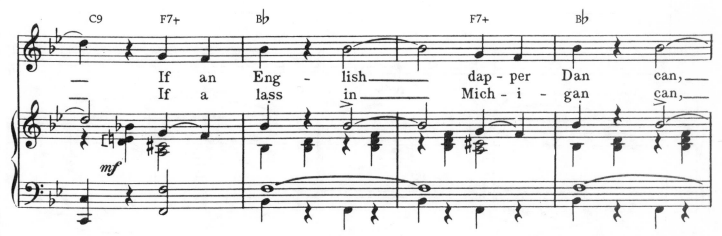

If an Eng - lish_____ dap - per Dan can,_____
If a lass in_____ Mich - i - gan can,_____

193

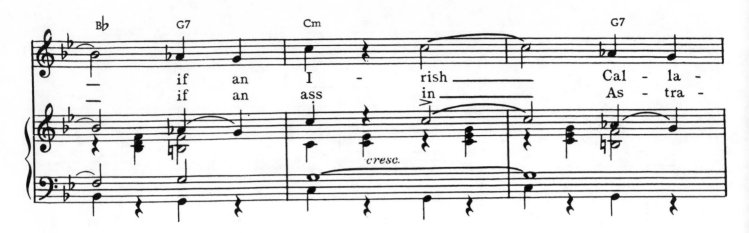

if an I - rish _____ Cal - la -
if an ass in _____ As - tra -

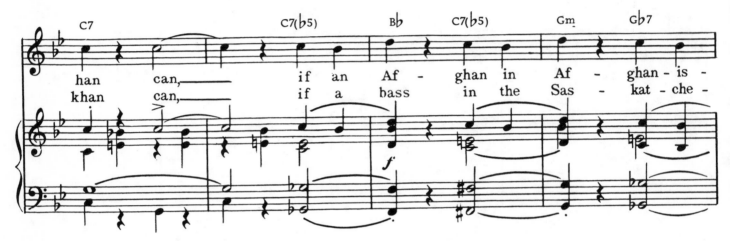

han can, _____ if an Af - ghan in Af - ghan - is -
khan can, _____ if a bass in the Sas - kat - che -

tan can, _____ Ba - by, you can Can - Can
wan* can, _____ Ba - by, you can Can - Can

1.
too. _____ 2. Takes no

2.
too. _____

*Pronounce to rhyme with Can.

194

CAN-CAN
Additional Lyrics

REFRAIN 3

If in Deauville ev'ry swell can,
It is so simple to do,
If Debussy and Ravel can,
'Twill be so easy for you.
If the Louvre custodian can,
If the Guard Republican can,
If Van Gogh and Matisse and Cézanne can,
Baby, you can can-can too.
If a chief in the Sudan can,
If the hefty Aga Khan can,
If the camels in his caravan can,
Baby, you can can-can too.

REFRAIN 4

If the waltz king Johann Strauss can,
It is so simple to do,
If his gals in *Fledermaus* can,
'Twill be so easy for you.
Lovely Duse in Milan can,
Lucien Guitry and Réjane can,
Sarah Bernhardt upon a divan can,
Baby, you can can-can too.
If a holy Hindu man can,
If a gangly Anglican can,
If in Lesbos, a pure Lesbian can,
Baby, you can can-can too.

REFRAIN 5

If an ape gargantuan can,
It is so simple to do,
If a clumsy pelican can,
'Twill be so easy for you.
If a dachshund in Berlin can,
If a tom-cat in Pekin can,
If a crowded sardine in a tin can,
Baby, you can can-can too.
If a rhino with a crash can,
If a hippo with a splash can,
If an elm and an oak and an ash can,
Baby, you can can-can too.

Shubert Theatre program cover for CAN-CAN (892 performances)

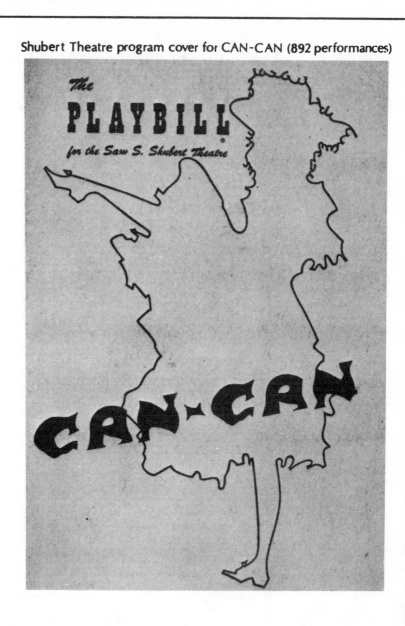

Abe Burrows, author of CAN-CAN's book and its director

I AM IN LOVE

COLE PORTER

Sit down, if you please and from laugh-ing re-frain, Sit down, if you

please, and I beg you try to lis-ten while I ex-plain:

REFRAIN (Moderate, steady fox-trot)

I am de-ject-ed, I am de-pressed,

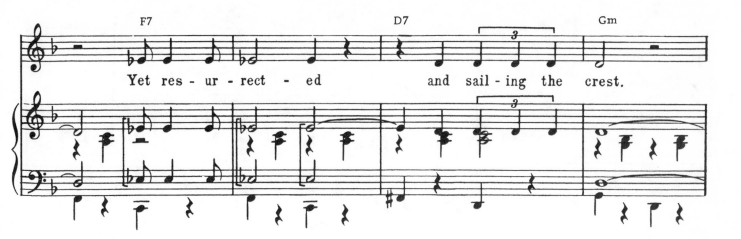

Yet res - ur - rect - ed and sail - ing the crest.

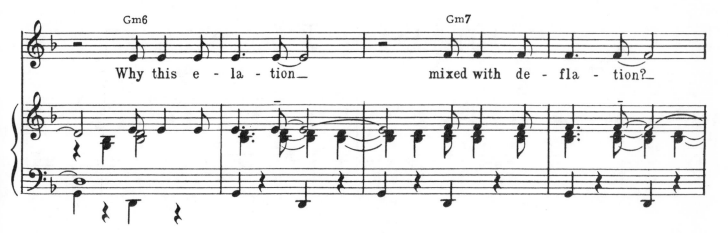

Why this e - la - tion___ mixed with de - fla - tion?___

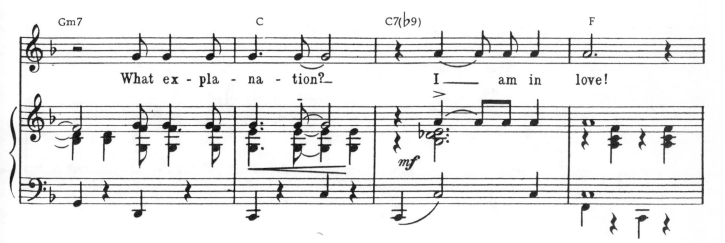

What ex - pla - na - tion?___ I___ am in love!

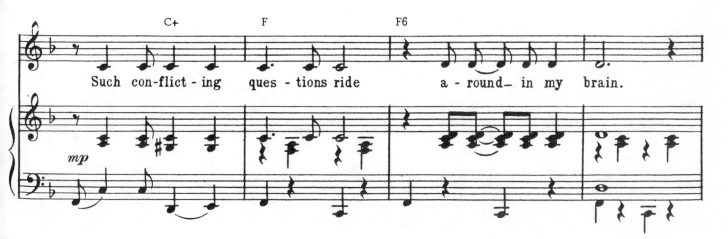

Such con - flict - ing ques - tions ride a - round___ in my brain.

Should I or-der cy - a-nide or or - der cham-pagne?

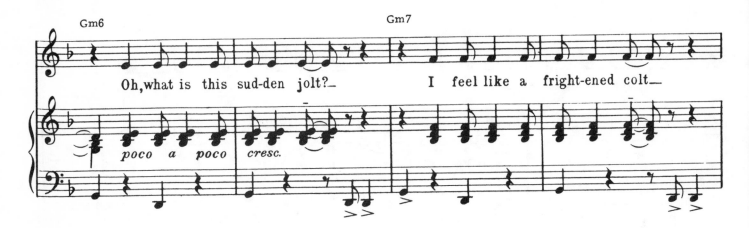

Oh, what is this sud-den jolt?__ I feel like a fright-ened colt__

just hit by a thun-der-bolt;__ I __ am in love!

I knew the odds were a - gainst me be - fore,

I had no flare for flam-ing de - sire,

But since the gods gave me you to a - dore,

I may lose, but I re - fuse to fight the fire!

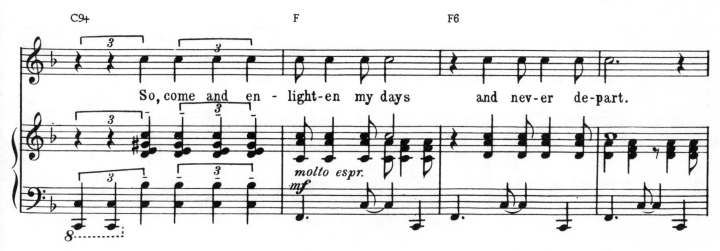

So, come and en - light-en my days and nev-er de-part.

You on-ly can bright-en the blaze that burns in my heart,

For I am wild ly in love with you

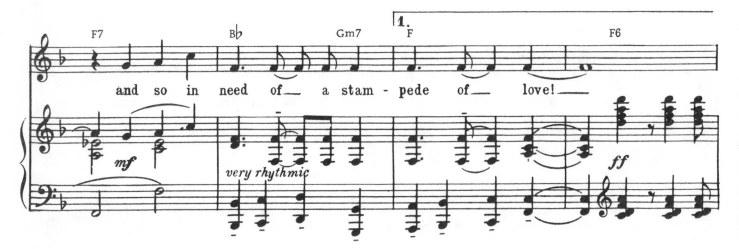

and so in need of_ a stam - pede of_ love!_

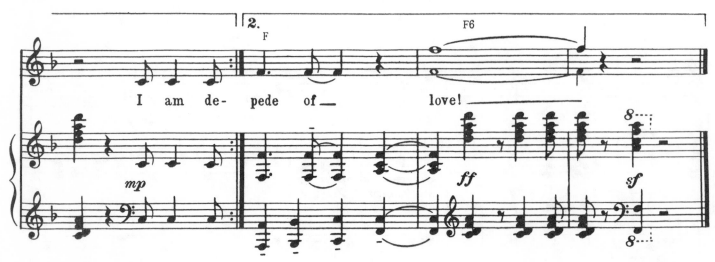

I am de- pede of_ love!_____

200

CAN-CAN

1. The dancers performing the "Quadrille" with the spicy, spirited choreography of Michael Kidd.

2. Chappell's sheet music title page for the movie version of CAN-CAN.

3. Gwen Verdon and Erik Rhodes.

I LOVE PARIS

COLE PORTER

Ev -'ry time I look down on this time - less town, wheth- er

blue or grey be her skies, Wheth - er

loud be her cheers, or wheth-er soft be her tears, more and

more — do I re - al - ize

poco rit.

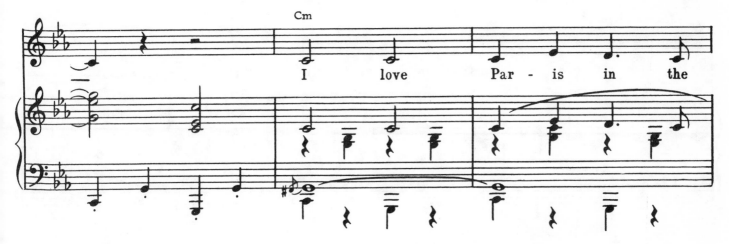

REFRAIN (Slow fox-trot tempo)

I love Par - is in the spring - time,__

p legato

I love Par - is in the

fall,__ I love

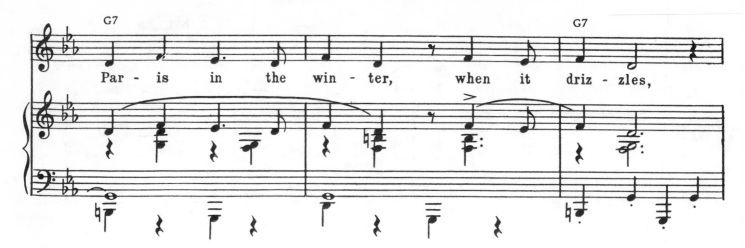

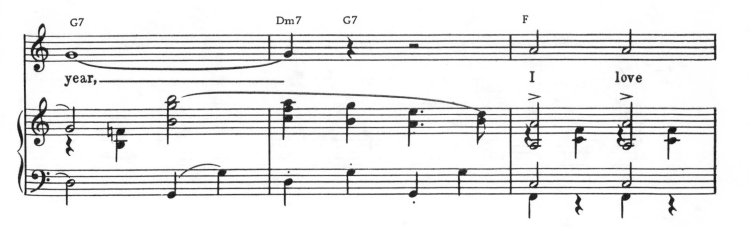

year,_____ I love

Par - is, why, oh why do I love Par - is?

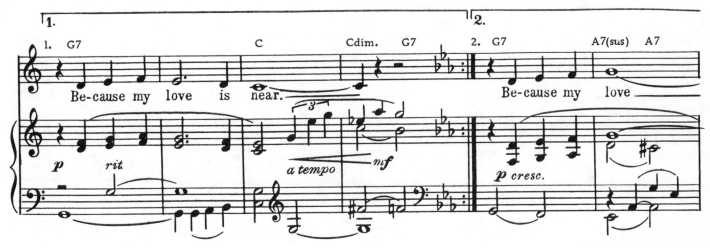

1. Be-cause my love is near. 2. Be-cause my love ___

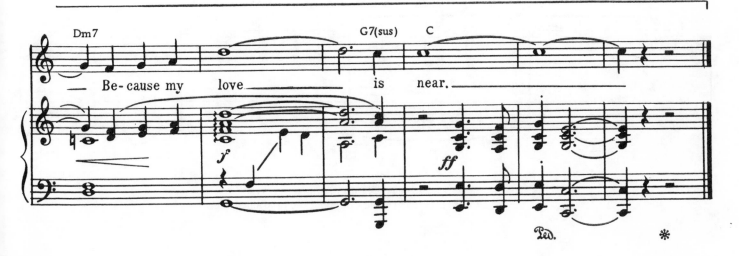

___ Be-cause my love ___ is near. ___

IT'S ALL RIGHT WITH ME

COLE PORTER

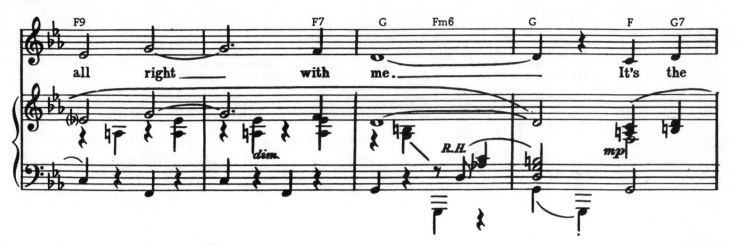

all right _____ with me. _____ It's the

wrong song _____ in the wrong style _____ tho' your

smile is love - ly, it's the wrong smile, _____ it's not

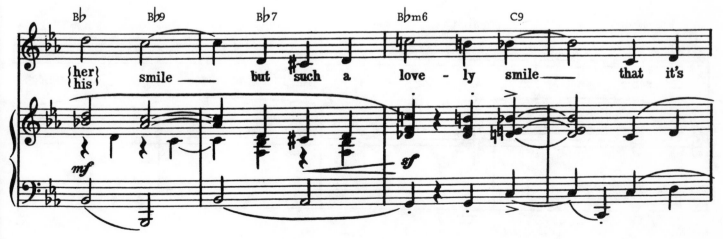

{her}
{his} smile _____ but such a love - ly smile _____ that it's

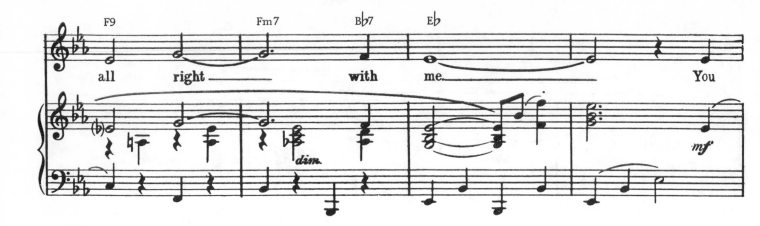

all right _____ with me. _____ You

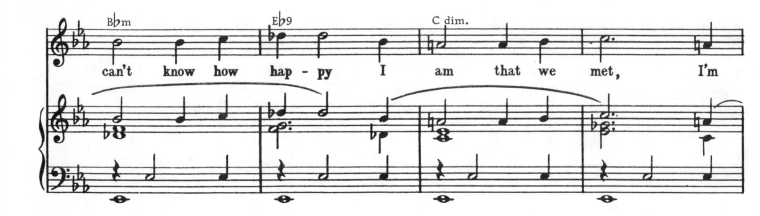

can't know how hap - py I am that we met, I'm

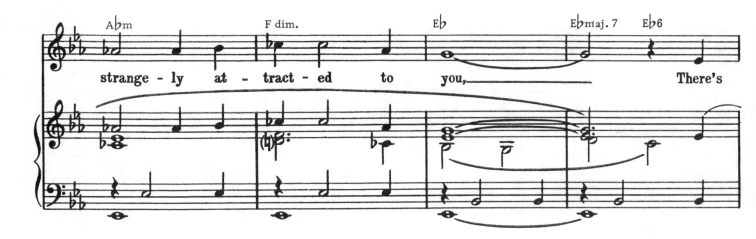

strange - ly at - tract - ed to you, _____ There's

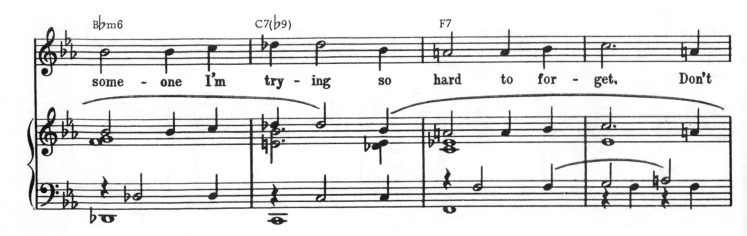

some - one I'm try - ing so hard to for - get. Don't

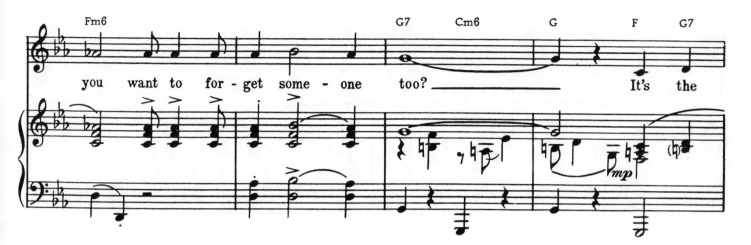

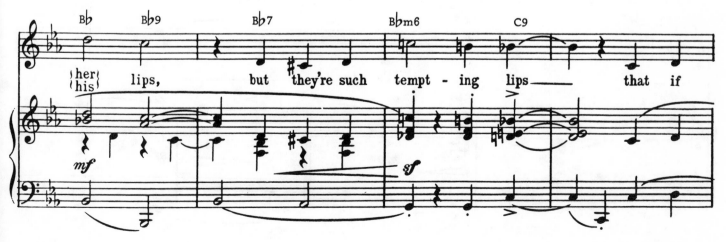

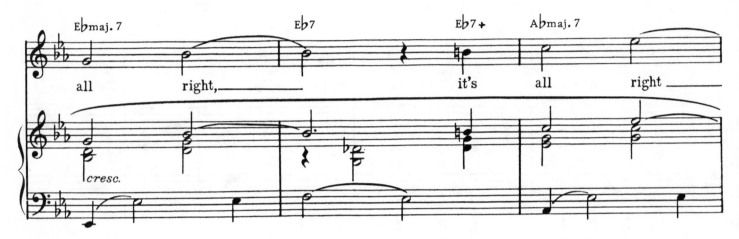

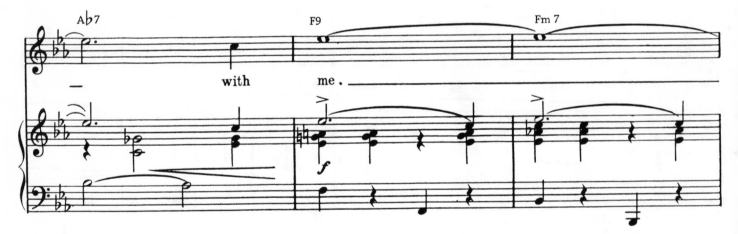

Silk Stockings

Produced by **CY FEUER & ERNEST MARTIN**

First performance: February 24, 1955 at the
Imperial Theatre, New York
playing for 427 performances

Music & Lyrics by **COLE PORTER**
Book by **GEORGE S. KAUFMAN, LEUEEN MacGRATH,**
and **ABE BURROWS**

Directed by **CY FEUER**
Dances & Musical Numbers staged by **EUGENE LORING**
Settings & Lighting by **JO MIELZINER**
Costumes by **LUCINDA BALLARD**
Musical Direction by **HERBERT GREENE**

The cast included:
Don Ameche, Hildegarde Neff, Gretchen Wyler,
George Tobias, Leon Belasco, Henry Lascoe, David
Opatoshu, and Philip Sterling

PARIS LOVES LOVERS

COLE PORTER

Gaze— on those glist-'ning lights be-

loward a-bove. Oh, what a night of nights for peo-ple in love.

No cit - y, but this, my friend, no cit - y, I know

Gives ro-mance such a chance to grow and grow.

preme, wake up your dream ——— and make love!"

That's an-ti-

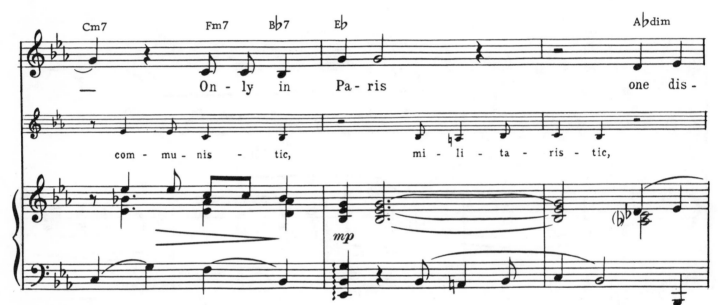

On - ly in Pa - ris   one dis-

com - mu - nis - tic,   mi - li - ta - ris - tic,

cov - ers   The urge to merge with the

You're op - ti - mis - tic.

splurge of the spring. _____

bour - geois pro - pa - gan - da!

Pa - ris loves lov - ers, For

un - re - al - is - tic.

lov - ers know that love is ev - 'ry -

SILK STOCKINGS in rehearsal
Above, left to right: Cole Porter, Leueen MacGrath, George S. Kaufman, Don Ameche, and Hildegarde Neff. Below, left to right: Ernest H. Martin and Cy Feuer, the producers, and George S. Kaufman: Seated: Leueen MacGrath and Cole Porter.

ALL OF YOU

COLE PORTER

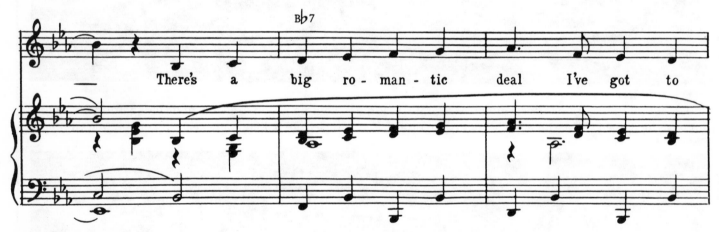

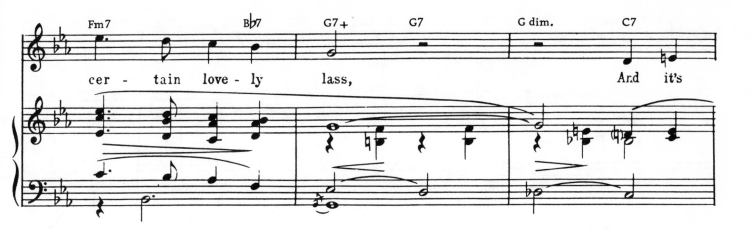

cer - tain love - ly   lass,   And it's

not a pass - ing fan - cy or a fan - cy pass.__

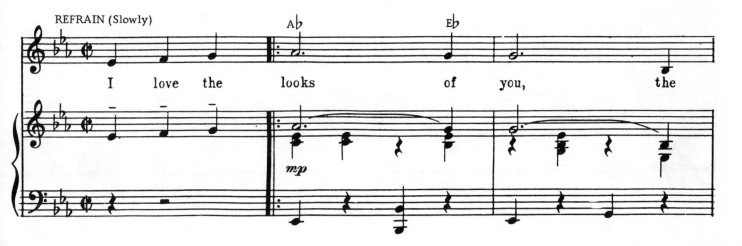

REFRAIN (Slowly)

I love the looks of you,   the

lure of you,   I'd love   to make a

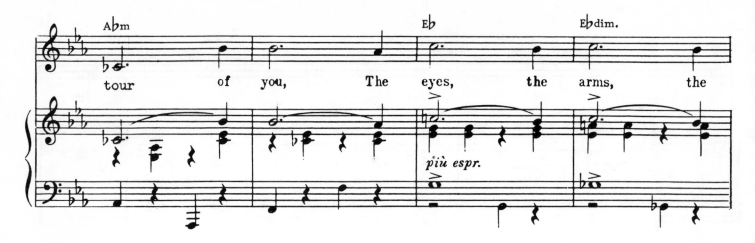

tour of you, The eyes, the arms, the

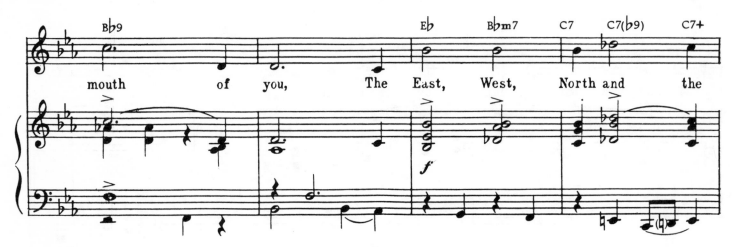

mouth of you, The East, West, North and the

South of you. _____ I'd love to gain com -

plete con - trol of you, And han - dle

e - ven the heart and soul of you, So

love, at least, a small per - cent__ of me, do,_____

For I love all of

You. I love the You._____

STEREOPHONIC SOUND

COLE PORTER

Steady, march tempo

REFRAIN

1. To - day to get the pub-lic to at - tend a pic-ture show It's
2. (You) all re-mem-ber Las-sie, that be - lov - ed ca-nine star. To

not e-nough to ad-ver-tise a fam-ous star they know. If you want to get the
see her wag her tail the crowds would come from near and far. But at pre-sent she'd be

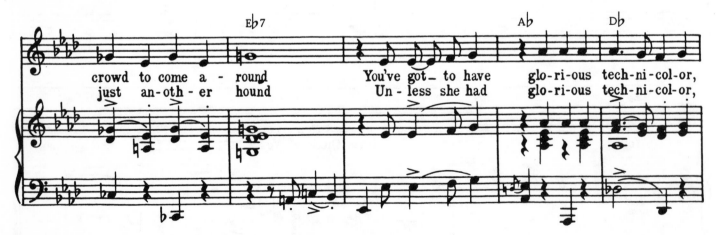

crowd to come a - round You've got— to have glo-ri-ous tech-ni-col-or,
just an-oth-er hound Un - less she had glo-ri-ous tech-ni-col-or,

Breath-tak - ing cin - e - ma-scope and Ste - re - o - phon - ic sound.
Breath-tak - ing cin - e - ma-scope and Ste - re - o - phon - ic sound.

If Zan - uck's la-test pic-ture were the
I late - ly did a pic-ture at the

good old-fash -ioned kind There'd be no - one in front to look at
bot - tom of the sea. I ras - sled with an oc - to-pus and

Mar - i -lyn's be - hind. If you want to hear ap - plaud-ing hands re-
licked an an - cho - vee. But the pub - lic would - n't care if I had

223

*sound,
drowned

You've got to have glorious tech-ni-col-or,
Un-less I had glorious tech-ni-col-or,

Breath-tak-ing cin-e-ma-scope and Ste-re-o-phon-ic sound.
Breath-tak-ing cin-e-ma-scope and Ste-re-o-phon-ic sound.

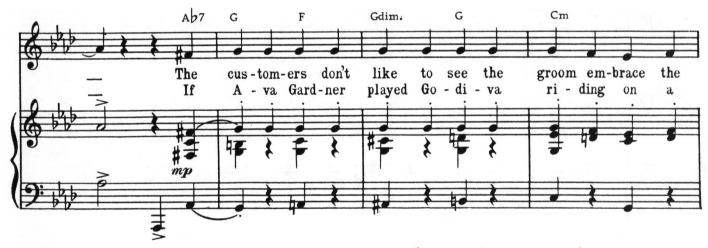

The cus-tom-ers don't like to see the groom em-brace the
If A-va Gard-ner played Go-di-va ri-ding on a

bride; Un-less her lips are scar-let and her mouth is five feet
mare, The peo-ple would-n't pay a cent and they would-n't e-ven

Pronounce "zound"

224

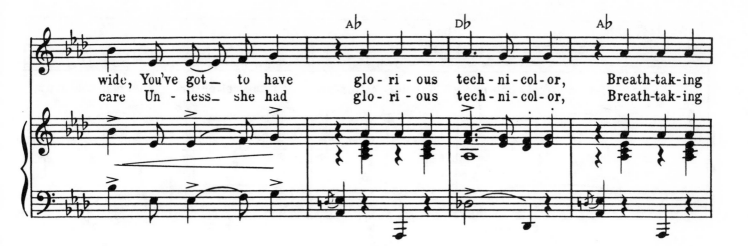

wide, You've got — to have   glo-ri-ous tech-ni-col-or, Breath-tak-ing
care Un-less_ she had   glo-ri-ous tech-ni-col-or, Breath-tak-ing

cin-e-ma-scope or Cin-e-ra-ma, Vis-ta-vi-sion, Su-per-scope or
cin-e-ma-scope or

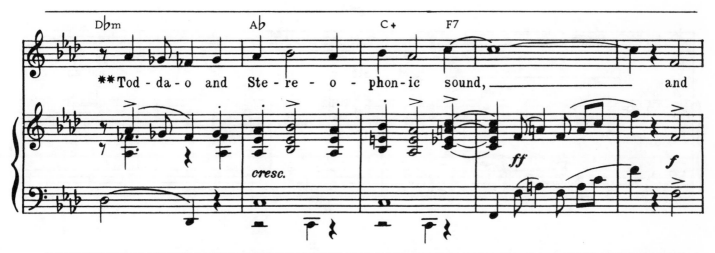

**Tod-da-o and Ste-re-o-phon-ic sound,_____ and

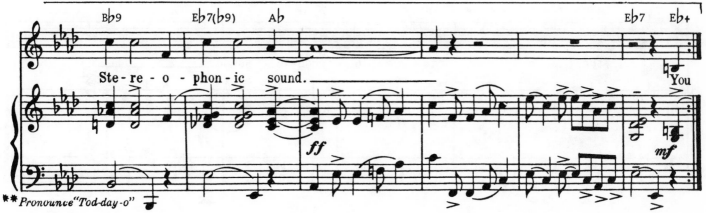

Ste-re-o-phon-ic sound._____ You

** Pronounce "Tod-day-o"

Cin - e - col-or or   War-ner - col-or or   Pa-thé-col-or or   East-man-col-or or

Ko - da - col-or or   an - y col-or and Ste - re - o - phon - ic   sound

and Ste - re - o - phon-ic   as an ex-tra

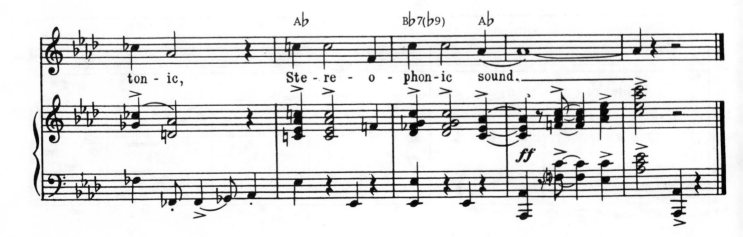

ton - ic,   Ste - re - o - phon-ic sound.

SILK STOCKINGS

1. Gretchen Wyler discovers Don Ameche and Hildegarde Neff in the joys of discovering one another. 2. Gretchen as "Josephine" with a cynical Napoleon watching the proceedings. 3 and 4. Hildegarde Neff and Don Ameche. SILK STOCKINGS was Cole Porter's last Broadway show and played 427 performances.

SIBERIA

COLE PORTER

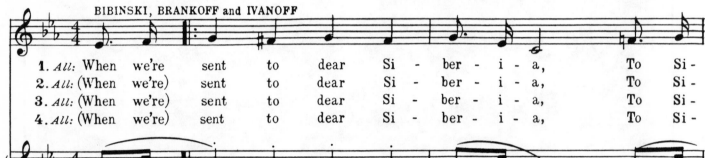

BIBINSKI, BRANKOFF and IVANOFF

1. *All:* When we're sent to dear Si - ber - i - a, To Si -
2. *All:* (When we're) sent to dear Si - ber - i - a, To Si -
3. *All:* (When we're) sent to dear Si - ber - i - a, To Si -
4. *All:* (When we're) sent to dear Si - ber - i - a, To Si -

ber - i - eer - i - a, When it's cock - tail time 'twill
ber - i - eer - i - a, Where they say all day the
ber - i - eer - i - a, Where the la - bor laws are
ber - i - eer - i - a, Since the big salt mines will

be so nice *(Ivanoff)* Just to know you'll not have to phone for ice, *(All)* When we
sun shines bright *(Ivanoff)* And they al - so say that it shines all night, *(All)* The au-
all so fair *(Ivanoff)* That you nev - er have un - em - ploy-ment there, *(All)* When we
be so near *(Ivanoff)* We can all have salt to put in our beer, *(All)* When we

meet in sweet Si - ber - i - a, Far from com - mun - ist hys-
ro - ra bor - e - al - is is Not as heat - ed as a
meet in sweet Si - ber - i - a, To pro - tect us from diph-
meet in sweet Si - ber - i - a, Where the snow is so su -

ter - i - a, *(Ivanoff)* We'll go on a tear, For our bud - dies all are there *(All)* In
pal-ace is, *(Ivanoff)* If on heat you dote, You can shoot a sa - ble coat *(All)* In
ther-i - a, *(Ivanoff)* We can toast our toes On the la - dy es - ki - mos *(All)* In
per-i - a,* *(Ivanoff)* You can bet, all right, That your Christ-mas will be white *(All)* In

*Superia meaning Superior.

cheer - y Si - ber - i - a
cheer - y Si - ber - i - a
cheer - y Si - ber - i - a
cheer - y Si - ber - i - a

1.

2.

a
a
a
a

2. *(All)* When we're
3. *(All)* When we're
4. *(All)* When we're

a

a.

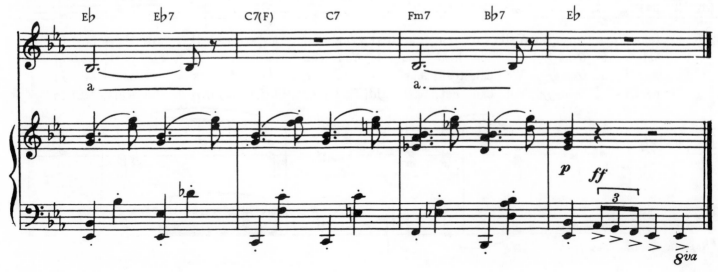

SILK STOCKINGS - Film
1. Fred Astaire and Cyd Charisse. 2. Sheet music title page 3. Janis Paige's performance of "Satin and Silk" works its charms on Wim Sonneveld.

SILK STOCKINGS

COLE PORTER

Dreamily, without dragging

So the dream was doomed to die, So it's o - ver,

dear, _____ And you sent a sweet good-bye

With a sou - ven - ir. _____ What a heart warm-ing

souvenir, For again you are there _____ On the

smiling night, When to my delight, I first saw you dare _____ wear

REFRAIN (in steady movement)

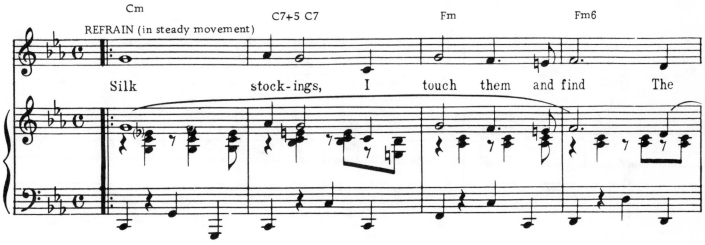

Silk stockings, I touch them and find The

joys that remind me of you. _____

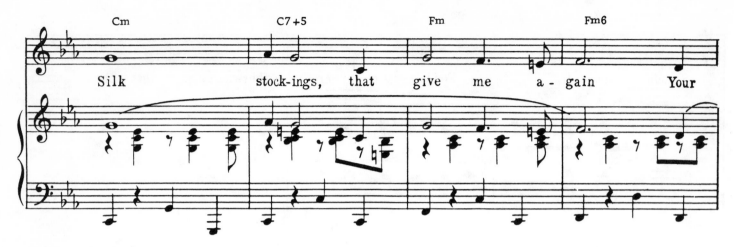

Silk stock-ings, that give me a - gain Your

shy laugh - ter when they were new.

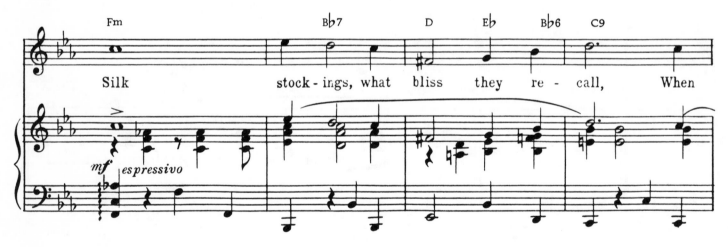

Silk stock-ings, what bliss they re - call, When

love prom-ised all for - ev - er - more. A pair of

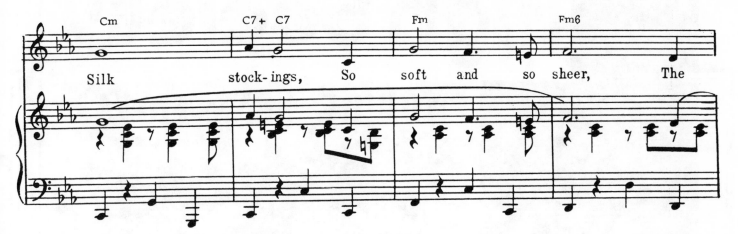

Silk stock-ings, So soft and so sheer, The

dear silk stock-ings_____ you

wore._____

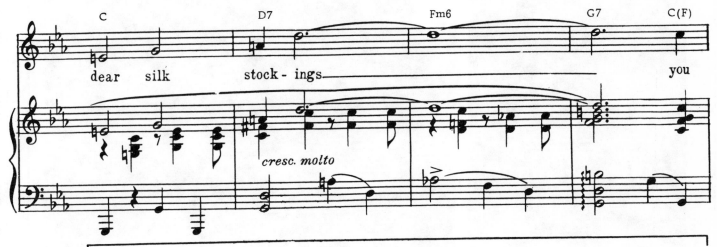

wore._____

High Society

An MGM Film

Produced by **SOL C. SIEGEL**

Released August 3, 1956

Music & Lyrics by **COLE PORTER**
Screenplay by **JOHN PATRICK**
based on Philip Barry's stage play
''The Philadelphia Story''

Directed by **CHARLES WALTERS**
Music Supervised & Adapted by **JOHNNY GREEN
& SAUL CHAPIN**

The cast included:
Bing Crosby, Grace Kelly, Frank Sinatra, Celeste
Holm, John Lund, Louis Calhern, Sidney Blackmer,
and Louis Armstrong

TRUE LOVE

COLE PORTER

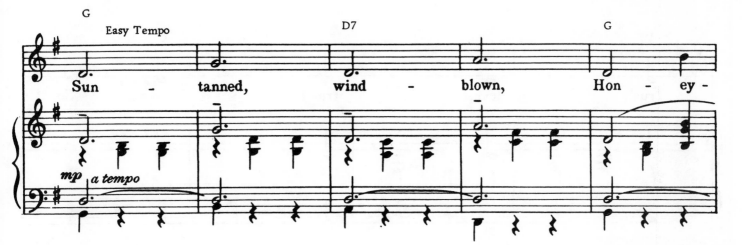

Sun - tanned, wind - blown, Hon - ey -

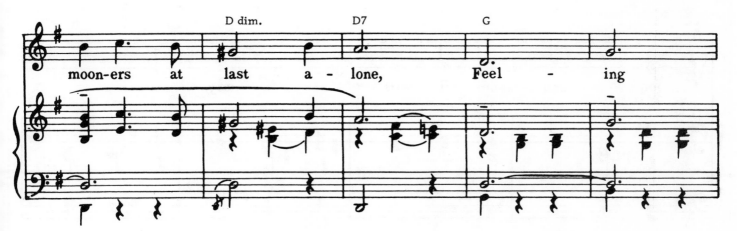

moon-ers at last a - lone, Feel - ing

far a - bove par. Oh, how luck-y we are. _____ While

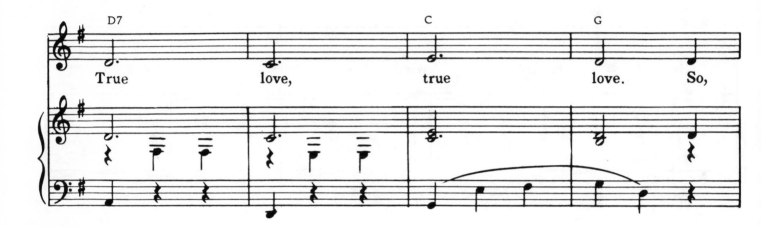

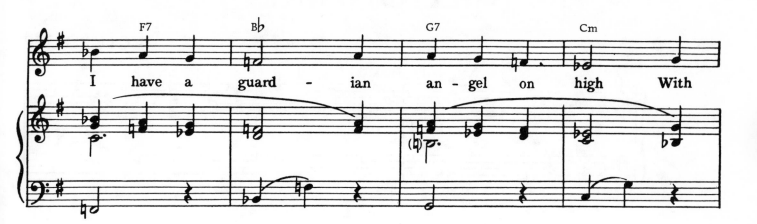

I have a guard - ian an - gel on high With

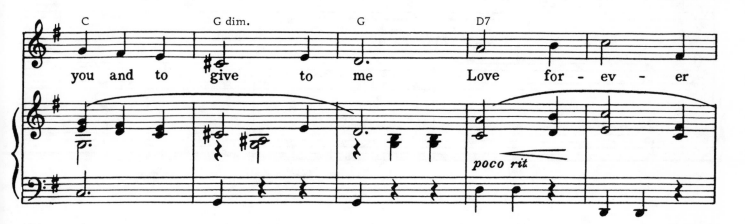

noth - ing to do _____ But to give to

you and to give to me Love for - ev - er

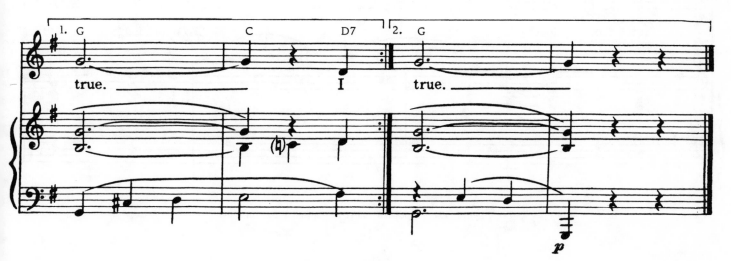

1. true. _____ I 2. true. _____

WHO WANTS TO BE A MILLIONAIRE?

COLE PORTER

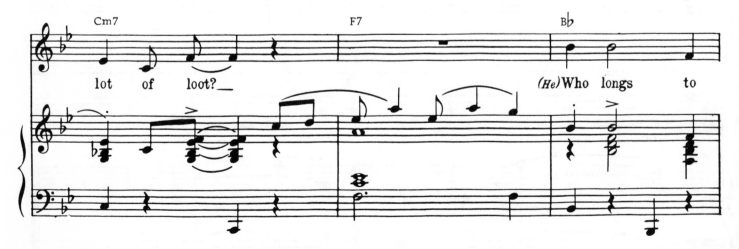

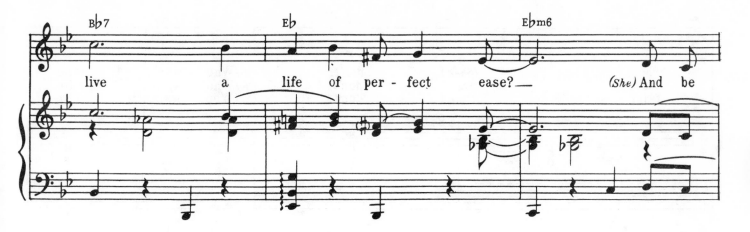

live   a   life   of per - fect   ease?___   (She) And be

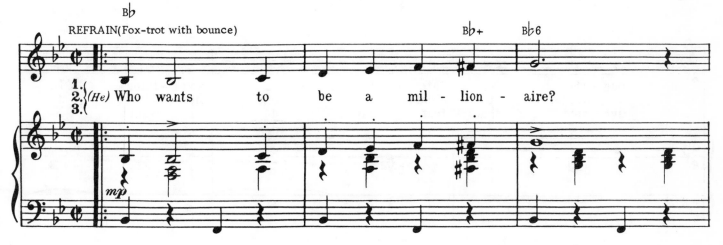

swamped   by ne - ces - sar - y   lux - ur - ies?___

REFRAIN(Fox-trot with bounce)

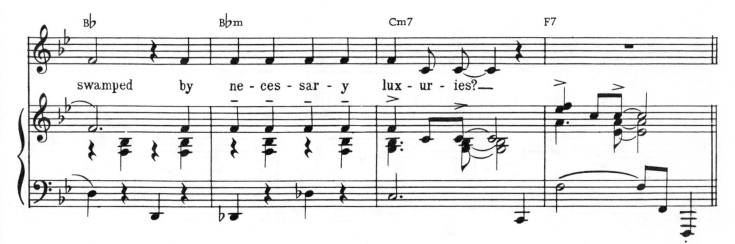

1.
2. (He) Who wants   to   be   a   mil - lion - aire?
3.

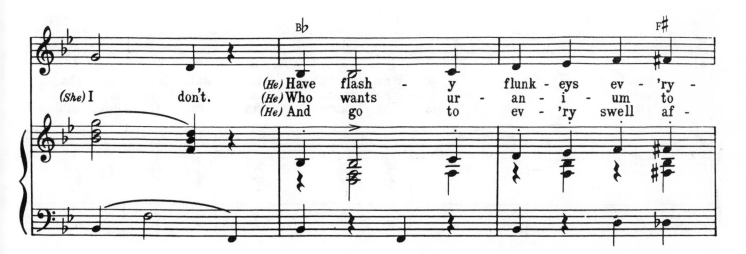

(She) I   don't.
(He) Have flash - y   flunk - eys ev - 'ry -
(He) Who wants   ur - an - i - um to
(He) And   go   to   ev - 'ry swell af -

pagne? *(She)* I don't. *(He)* Who wants a su - per - son - ic
car? *(He)* I don't. *(She)* Who wants to tire of cav - i -
bet? *(She)* I don't. *(She)* And sleep through Wag - ner at the

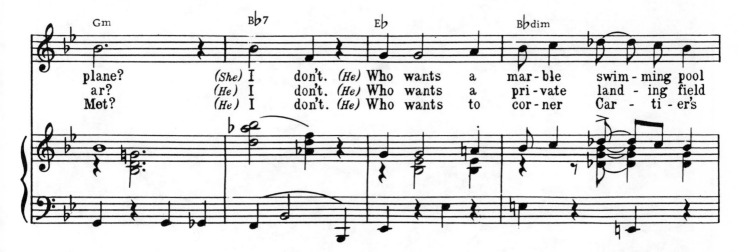

plane? *(She)* I don't. *(He)* Who wants a mar - ble swim - ming pool
ar? *(He)* I don't. *(He)* Who wants a pri - vate land - ing field
Met? *(He)* I don't. *(He)* Who wants to cor - ner Car - ti - er's

too?
too? *(She)* I don't, *(He)* and I don't, *(Both)* 'cause all I want is you._
too?

HIGH SOCIETY

1. Grace Kelly and Bing Crosby sang "True Love" which received an Oscar nomination as best song but failed to win. Porter was not surprised - he felt it to be one of his poorer songs. 2. Frank Sinatra and Bing trade quips in "Well, Did you Evah!" 3. Louis "Satchmo" Armstrong and Bing in "Now You Has Jazz."

Les Girls

An MGM Film

Produced by **SOL C. SIEGEL**

Released in November, 1957

Music & Lyrics by **COLE PORTER**
Screenplay by **JOHN PATRICK**
based on a story by Vera Caspary

Associate Producer **SAUL CHAPLIN**
Directed by **GEORGE CUKOR**
Music Adapted & Conducted by **ADOLPH DEUTSCH**
Choreography by **JACK COLE**

The cast included:
Gene Kelly, Mitzi Gaynor, Kay Kendall,
and Taina Elg

LES GIRLS

COLE PORTER

Lyrics:
'Round the map I've been a dan-cer From New Jer-sey to Ja-pan, And if not a per-fect pran-cer, I'm at

least a tip-top tra-vel-in' man.__ Yes, I've played ad in-fin-

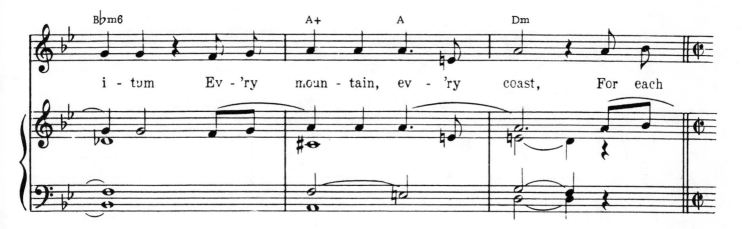

i-tum Ev-'ry moun-tain, ev-'ry coast, For each

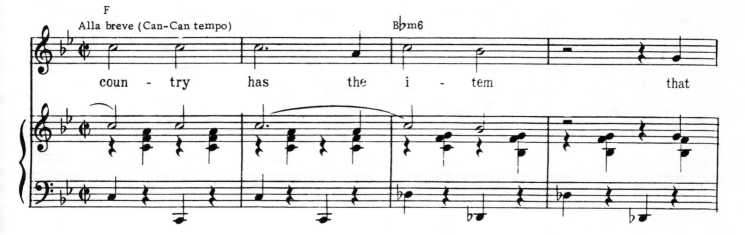

coun - try has the i - tem that

I en - joy the most.

REFRAIN (Can-Can tempo)

Les Girls, _____ Les Girls, _____ There's no doubt a-

bout it, I just love Les Girls! Les Girls, _____ Les

Girls, _____ No won - der I shout it, I

wor - ship Les Girls! Ah, what charms they dis - close From their

hats to their hose, From the tips of their toes up to their

curls, _____ I simp - ly a - dore, And

ev - 'ry day more, Les Girls, Les Girls, Les

1.
Girls. _____ Les Girls.

2.

LES GIRLS
1. Taina Elg, Kay Kendall and Mitzi Gaynor 2. Gene Kelly and Kay Kendall in
''You're Just Too, Too.'' 3. Mitzi Gaynor and Kay Kendall 4. A battle of
affections ensues in court between Taina Elg (seated) and Kay Kendall (stand-
ing). 5. Gene Kelly

Aladdin

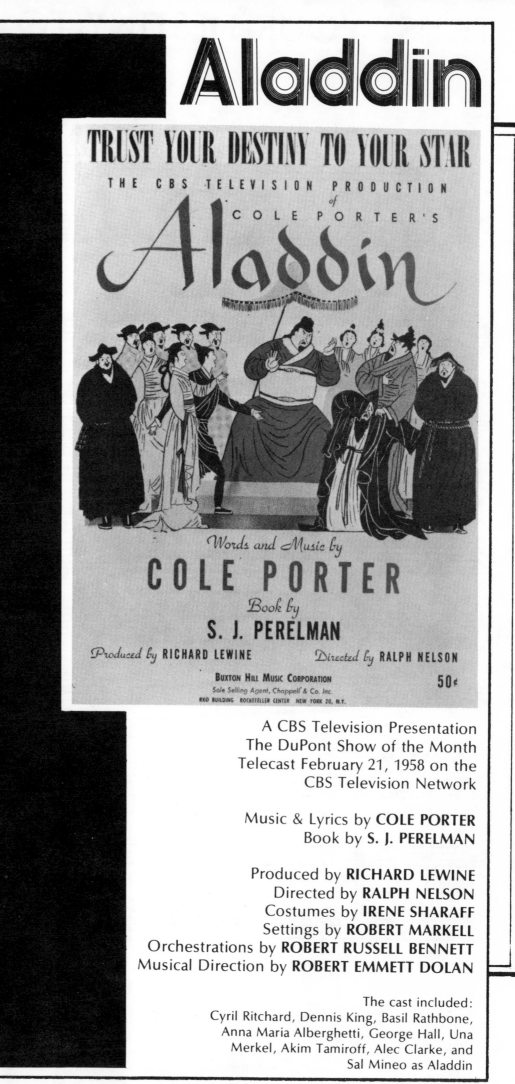

A CBS Television Presentation
The DuPont Show of the Month
Telecast February 21, 1958 on the
CBS Television Network

Music & Lyrics by **COLE PORTER**
Book by **S. J. PERELMAN**

Produced by **RICHARD LEWINE**
Directed by **RALPH NELSON**
Costumes by **IRENE SHARAFF**
Settings by **ROBERT MARKELL**
Orchestrations by **ROBERT RUSSELL BENNETT**
Musical Direction by **ROBERT EMMETT DOLAN**

The cast included:
Cyril Ritchard, Dennis King, Basil Rathbone,
Anna Maria Alberghetti, George Hall, Una
Merkel, Akim Tamiroff, Alec Clarke, and
Sal Mineo as Aladdin

TRUST YOUR DESTINY TO A STAR

COLE PORTER

des - ti - ny to your star._____ If you

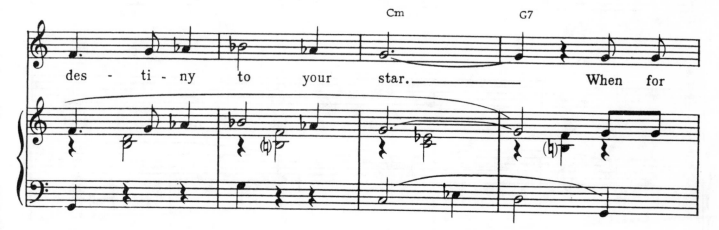

long for glo - ry and fame un - told, Trust your

des - ti - ny to your star._____ When for

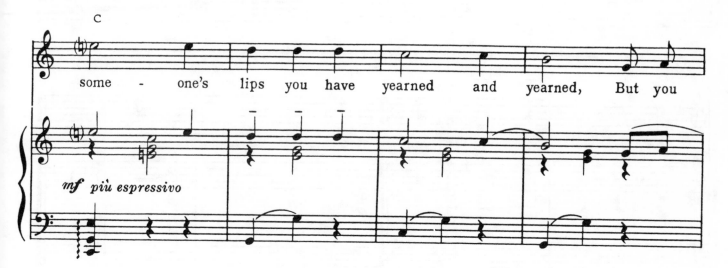

some - one's lips you have yearned and yearned, But you

mf più espressivo

live with-out hope so far, _____ You will

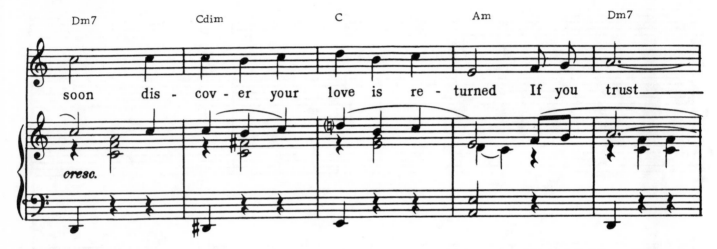

soon dis-cov-er your love is re-turned If you trust_____

__ And you must_____ Trust your des-ti-ny to your

1. STAR. If you

2. star._____

255

SHOW/FILM INDEX